The Economics of Gender and the Household in Developing Countries

# DEVELOPMENT ECONOMICS AND POLICY

Series edited by Franz Heidhues, Joachim von Braun and Manfred Zeller

Vol. 60

PETER LANG

Frankfurt am Main · Berlin · Bern · Bruxelles · New York · Oxford · Wien

# The Economics of Gender and the Household in Developing Countries

Holger Seebens

PETER LANG
Internationaler Verlag der Wissenschaften

**Bibliographic Information published by the Deutsche Nationalbibliothek**
The Deutsche Nationalbibliothek lists this publication in the Deutsche Nationalbibliografie; detailed bibliographic data is available in the internet at <http://www.d-nb.de>.

Zugl.: Göttingen, Univ., Diss., 2007

D 7
ISSN 0948-1338
ISBN 978-3-631-54649-9
© Peter Lang GmbH
Internationaler Verlag der Wissenschaften
Frankfurt am Main 2009
All rights reserved.

All parts of this publication are protected by copyright. Any utilisation outside the strict limits of the copyright law, without the permission of the publisher, is forbidden and liable to prosecution. This applies in particular to reproductions, translations, microfilming, and storage and processing in electronic retrieval systems.

www.peterlang.de

For Matjes and Biko who suffered most and
for Inge and Dieter for constant support.

## Acknowledgement

This study would not have been possible without the support of many people. Most importantly I am grateful to my supervisor Prof. Stephan Klasen who constantly provided input and support. I also would like to thank the other members of the examination committee Prof. Michael Grimm and Prof. Matin Qaim who both immediately agreed to join the board. For financial support I am thankful to the Robert Bosch Foundation which enabled the operation of the PASAD project under whose umbrella I was conducting my research. The project leader Dr. Peter Wobst was always challenging, but never got tired to provide guidance and help. I am particularly grateful for him facilitating and supporting my international exposure.

International exposure entailed several visits at the International Food Policy Research Institute (IFPRI), where Dr. Agnes Quisumbing and Dr. John Hoddinott were always willing to take some of their scarce time to read and comment on my papers. Although they were causing the one and other small crisis, without their support I would not have been able to pursue my research. In this regard I am particularly grateful to Agnes for inviting me to Boston and for providing me with data and STATA codes that saved me lots of work. My stays at IFPRI would not have been so pleasant without James Thurlow who was hosting me most of times and who had to stand my confusions.

Most of this work was written while being at the Center of Development Research (ZEF) of the University of Bonn where constant exchange with fellow PhD students and staff members provided an inspiring environment. Here, I particularly would like to thank my room mates Alexander Stein and Ricardo Guimaraes with whom I had a great and funny as well as serious working time. Also, Jan Börner and Marc Müller were always open for challenging discussions. Without their support, I would probably still fix problems on production and cost functions. Although he might not be aware of, Prof. Arnab Basu was teaching me more economic theory through his input, comments and the discussions at the ZEF kitchen than I ever learnt at the University. He also substantially contributed through his input to the success of this study. I also would like to thank Florian Scholtes and Nicolas Gerber for proof reading and commenting on the many final drafts.

In Tanzania, many friends and colleagues were supportive. Here, I would like to mention particularly David Nyange from Sokoine University of Agriculture in Morogoro who facilitated and enabled my research stay. Also, without the help from Abdallah Mrinji who guided me through the difficulties of field research. The contact came about with the help from John Mduma with whom I worked in the PASAD project together with Borbala Balint and Hardwick Tchale. I particularly grateful to Dr. Nancy Nafula from the Kenyan Institute for Public Policy Research and Analysis (KIPPRA) for helping me out with the full set of the WMS III questionnaires. Finally, I would like to thank the colleageus and staff at ZEF and the many people who have accompanied the process of writing this book and who are not explicitly mentioned.

## Foreword of the editors

Women in developing countries contribute a major share to the wellbeing of all members of society. In particular, women in sub-Saharan Africa are often seen as the main providers of food in agricultural households and further earn a share of household cash income. Moreover, besides being economically productive, women do most of the work with respect to child care and labor recreation. In view of this, it is important to ask how women fare in comparison to men. The answer to this question bears consequences not only for women, but for other household members as well. Increasing incomes of women has been shown to be not only beneficial for the earning woman, but there are well documented spill-over effects to the welfare of children as well. For example, women who earn their own money, tend to spend more on food resulting in potentially better nourished children.

Although a recent body of research addresses many of the issues related to gender inequality and its implications, many questions still remain open. This study focuses on gender issues related to developing countries and thus contributes to and extends the numerous literatures on gender inequality. Much of the recent discussion has focused on women per se, without considering that these may not be a homogenous group as implicitly assumed. Although some studies have attempted to categorize female headed households into several subgroups and applied these categories to the analysis of poverty, this has never been done in the context of agricultural production, where being a female headed household is probably much more relevant as in poverty analysis, which rather reflects the different production circumstances.

The analysis of gender issues in this study is not restricted to comparing female and male headed households but extends to household decision making of married couples as well. In this context, the unitary household model often proves insufficient to appropriately describe household demand and decision making. This is particularly obvious when it is coming to fertility related decisions which have been rarely directly addressed in the development economics literature in terms of individual contributions to the final decision. The study's contribution lies also in the application of recent developments of econometric techniques that are more flexible and allow for deeper insights than the approaches that have been used in the past. The control for unobserved variables, e.g. through latent class models, is necessary particularly with respect to the analysis of fertility where modelling with covariates can be sometimes hazardous due to omitted variables.

Non-parametric and semi-parametric methods are perfectly suited for the analysis of demand, which is demonstrated in the chapter on the relation between demand for food and adult goods and child welfare. Similar methods have been developed to estimate adult equivalence scales. The results of this study, however, suggest that due to different patterns of demand among female and male headed households, these equivalence scales cannot be identified from usual household demand data.

The aim of this study is to shed new light on old questions and to demonstrate that some issues that seem to have found an answer involve more complexity as has been taken yet into consideration. Answering these questions can substantially help to promote development policies that not only lend support to increase the welfare of women but that create side effects for the good of family and society.

Prof. Dr. Joachim von Braun
International Food Policy Research Institute (IFPRI)
Washington D.C.

Prof. Dr. Franz Heidhues
Center for Tropical Agriculture
University of Hohenheim

Prof. Dr. Manfred Zeller
Institute of Agricultural Economics and Social Sciences in the Tropics and Subtropics
University of Hohenheim

## Contents

**1 Introduction**    **1**

**2 One size fits all? Female headed households and access to resources in Kenya**    **6**
- 2.1 Introduction . . . . . . . . . . . . . . . . . . . . . . . . . . 6
- 2.2 The problem of classifying FHH . . . . . . . . . . . . . . . 8
- 2.3 The model . . . . . . . . . . . . . . . . . . . . . . . . . . . 11
- 2.4 The data . . . . . . . . . . . . . . . . . . . . . . . . . . . . 18
- 2.5 Empirical implementation . . . . . . . . . . . . . . . . . . 20
  - 2.5.1 Constructing a test for the relevance of the four cases for the different FHH categories . . . . . . . . . . . . . . 20
- 2.6 Specification of the empirical model . . . . . . . . . . . . . 23
- 2.7 Estimation the of stochastic frontier cost function . . . . . . . . 26
- 2.8 Conclusions . . . . . . . . . . . . . . . . . . . . . . . . . . 32
- A Appendix 2.1 . . . . . . . . . . . . . . . . . . . . . . . . . 34

**3 Bargaining over Fertility in Rural Ethiopia**    **36**
- 3.3 Introduction . . . . . . . . . . . . . . . . . . . . . . . . . . 36
- 3.3 Fertility in Ethiopia—the setting . . . . . . . . . . . . . . . 39
- 3.3 Methodological Problems of Analyzing Determinants of Fertility 40
- 3.3 Birth Spacing . . . . . . . . . . . . . . . . . . . . . . . . . 41
  - 3.3.1 The Model . . . . . . . . . . . . . . . . . . . . . . 41
- 3.3 Unobserved Heterogeneity . . . . . . . . . . . . . . . . . . 43
- 3.3 Estimation . . . . . . . . . . . . . . . . . . . . . . . . . . 44
- 3.3 Results . . . . . . . . . . . . . . . . . . . . . . . . . . . . 47
- 3.3 Number of Children . . . . . . . . . . . . . . . . . . . . . 49
  - 3.3.1 The Model and Estimation . . . . . . . . . . . . . . 49
  - 3.3.2 Results . . . . . . . . . . . . . . . . . . . . . . . . 51
- 3.3 Conclusions . . . . . . . . . . . . . . . . . . . . . . . . . . 53
- A Appendix 3.1. . . . . . . . . . . . . . . . . . . . . . . . . 55

**4 Patterns of consumption and child welfare in female headed households in Tanzania**    **61**
- 4.4 Introduction . . . . . . . . . . . . . . . . . . . . . . . . . . 61
- 4.4 The old-age security motive for investing in children . . . . . . . 63
- 4.4 The data . . . . . . . . . . . . . . . . . . . . . . . . . . . . 65
- 4.4 Comparison of regression curves . . . . . . . . . . . . . . . 66
  - 4.4.1 Empirical approach . . . . . . . . . . . . . . . . . . 66
  - 4.4.2 Estimates of the Engel curves . . . . . . . . . . . . 71
  - 4.4.3 Testing for shape equality . . . . . . . . . . . . . . 73

|  |  |  |
|---|---|---|
| | 4.4.4 Household expenditure and children | 77 |
| 4.4 | The old-age security hypothesis | 80 |
| 4.4 | Conclusions | 82 |
| A | Appendix 4.1 | 85 |
| B | Appendix 4.2 | 93 |

**5 Food demand, female headed households, and the estimation of equivalence scales**     **95**

| | | |
|---|---|---|
| 5.5 | Introduction | 95 |
| 5.5 | The estimation of equivalence scales | 96 |
| 5.5 | Difference of demand across FHH and MHH | 101 |
| 5.5 | Food expenditure and children | 103 |
| 5.5 | Conclusions | 105 |

**6 Summary and conclusions**     **108**

**References**     **111**

# List of Tables

| | | |
|---|---|---|
| 1 | Different cases with missing labor markets | 16 |
| 2 | Different classes of FHH and their associated levels of bargaining power | 20 |
| 3 | Shares of FHH categories and resource endowment | 21 |
| 4 | Assignment of cases to FHH categories and expected signs of estimates | 23 |
| 5 | Estimates of production efficiency of different FHH categories | 28 |
| 6 | Estimates of production efficiency of single FHH indicator | 29 |
| 7 | Labor supply and shares of income generating households | 30 |
| 8 | Estimates of production efficiency of different FHH categories using dummy variables only | 31 |
| 9 | Estimates of the cost function parameters | 34 |
| 10 | Means and descriptions of variables | 55 |
| 11 | Jointly estimated parameters of all parities | 56 |
| 12 | Jointly estimated parameters of all parities and quit probabilities after third birth | 57 |
| 13 | Poisson model | 59 |
| 14 | Negative binomial model | 59 |
| 15 | Two-component count model of no. of child | 60 |
| 16 | Summary statistics | 85 |
| 17 | Shares of households purchasing goods | 85 |
| 18 | Estimated scale and shift parameters* | 86 |
| 19 | Estimated expenditure elasticities | 86 |
| 20 | Wald test for difference of parameters | 86 |
| 21 | Parameters of the semiparametric model - Food | 87 |
| 22 | Parameters of the semiparametric model - Clothing | 88 |
| 23 | Parameters of the semiparametric model - Education | 88 |
| 24 | Parameters of the semiparametric model - Tobacco | 89 |
| 25 | Parameters of the semiparametric model - Alcohol | 89 |
| 26 | First stage probit models - Clothing and education | 90 |
| 27 | First stage probit models - Alcohol and tobacco | 91 |
| 28 | Parameters of the old age model - food and education | 92 |
| 29 | Parameters of the semiparametric model - Food | 104 |

## List of Figures

| | | |
|---|---|---|
| 1 | Effects of $\theta$ on labor allocation | 15 |
| 2 | Effects of $p$ on labor allocation | 16 |
| 3 | Food budget shares for FHH and MHH | 72 |
| 4 | Budget shares for clothing in FHH and MHH | 73 |
| 5 | Budget shares for education in FHH and MHH | 74 |
| 6 | Budget shares for alcohol in FHH and MHH | 75 |
| 7 | Budget shares for tobacco in FHH and MHH | 76 |
| 8 | Food demand curves for savers and non-savers | 82 |
| 9 | Education demand curves for savers and non-savers | 83 |
| 10 | Identification of Engel equivalence scales | 99 |
| 11 | Identification of Engel equivalence scales | 100 |
| 12 | Food budget shares for FHH and MHH | 103 |
| 13 | Food budget shares for FHH of different sizes | 105 |
| 14 | Food budget shares for MHH of different sizes | 106 |

# 1 Introduction

Research on gender issues has long been on the agenda of development researchers, gaining increased attention with the work of Ester Boserup (1970) who emphasized the importance of women for economic development. However, the status of women in developing countries is often precarious as women are deprived in many respects. Women often have only few control over productive resources which renders them vulnerable to shocks like widowhood or implies difficulties in obtaining credits that often require a collateral (Migot-Adholla, Hazell, Blarel and Place 1991).

Gender gaps are visible in many different areas ranging from education, formal sector employment, to lacking political participation and representation. Although most countries have progressed in terms of education and successfully increased school enrollment and literacy rates over the past years, statistics from many countries still reveal a substantial educational gender gap. While South Asia and sub-Sahara Africa exhibit the lowest overall educational achievement, they also reveal the highest gender inequality in education (Blackden, Canagarajah, Klasen and Lawson 2006). Employment in the formal sector is mostly dominated by men where, again, South Asia and sub-Sahara Africa, but also Northern Africa and the Middle East exhibit particularly low female employment rates (Klasen and Lamanna 2003). Also, women tend to be underrepresented in political decision making. Blackden and Bhanu (1999) report that in Africa on average only 10 percent of the positions at local level legislatures are filled with women. Although these numbers can only illustrate a dimensions where gender gaps are present, they highlight the substantial inequality that is still taking place in the world.

Gender and development can be approached from two different angles: (i) Gender inequality, that refers to the several forms of deprivation of women (see Blackden and Bhanu 1999, Blackden et al. 2006, Ellis, Blackden, Cutura, MacCulloch and Seebens 2007, for a review of different dimensions of gender inequality in Africa). (ii) Preference heterogeneity, which takes into account that women and men have different preferences regarding the consumption of goods or the optimal number of desired children. Both areas are important fields of research and may even be interlinked. Both issues are addressed in this study.

Gender inequality is grounded in the institutional environment that defines power relations and leeways within which individuals can operate and which thus determine personal gains and benefits. Institutions can be informal as for instance traditions that define marriage and inheritance rules which assign individuals different control rights over resources. Structural inequality—i.e. institutionally fixed inequality—also finds its expression in legal norms as in the case of Tanzania, where article 59 of the Law of Marriage Act states that wives are not allowed to sell a house without permission of their husband, even if it is legally their property. Although in many sub-Sahara African countries, formal law aims at gender equity, the coexistence of two legal systems—customary and statutory law—effectively inhibits women from exercising their rights. Particularly in rural areas, customary law is predominantly applied which for example has led to an unclear definition of land rights as in many sub-Sahara African countries women are allowed to possess and sell land, while customary law prohibits it (Bruce and Migot-Adholla 1994).

However, such structural inequality reaches beyond the individual and has implications for economic development. For example Klasen (2002) has demonstrated that gender inequality in schooling significantly reduces economic growth. The investigation of detrimental effects resulting from the multidimensional deprivation of girls and women is therefore not only a pressing question on moral grounds but has further consequences that are directly measurable in terms of loss of income for the economy as a whole.

Research on gender is not restricted to inequality but extends to preferences of women and men. A substantial literature has been built on the preference structures across gender establishing significantly different consumption profiles of women and men (see Beegle, Frankenberg and Thomas 2001, Hoddinott and Haddad 1995, Haddad 1999). On average, women spend more on food compared to men which is empirically established in chapter 4 (see also Maluccio and Quisumbing 1999). Regarding fertility, various volumes of the final report of the Demographic and Health Survey (DHS) from different countries from the developing world reveal that men tend to prefer more children than women (see Bankole and Singh (1998) for an overview of the results from 13 different DHS data sets).

The purchase of goods or the decision on fertility goals are considerations to be made within the household which concern both women and men. Thus a couple needs to define the process according to which they want to arrive at a decision. The scope of this process can range from pure tyranny to perfect joint decision making where each individual has equal say. The household is therefore a place where the two areas of gender research—gender inequality and differing preferences—come together as two individuals with their own set of preferences enter a union which is partly guided by altruism and partly by selfish behavior.

To conduct research on household decisions it is therefore necessary to first identify the preference structure of different household members and secondly to analyze the decision making process given preferences. To what extent altruism or egoism prevail, that is, whether household decision making is dominated by a single person or made jointly is an empirical question. However, a number of studies have found that individual members dominate household decision making (see Lawrence Haddad and Alderman (1997), Behrman (1997) and Quisumbing (2003) for an extensive overview of the literature). Depending on whether men's or women's preferences prevail, household decision making turned out to be quite different with implications for the welfare of individual household members as well as on household outcomes in terms of production and demand for goods. An important result of this literature is that couples often do not pool incomes. This has far reaching consequences: household members do not fully insure each other against income shortfalls as has been found by Doss (1996) for the case of Ghana and by Duflo and Udry (2004) using data from Côte d'Ivoire. Goldstein (1999) finds that household members in Ghana find insurance outside the household rather than within. Udry (1996) establishes that farm households in Burkina Faso could significantly increase their production and hence their incomes if resources were allocated more equally and efficiently among household members. In all these cases households do not achieve Pareto efficiency in that at least one household member could be made better off without decreasing welfare of any other member. When structural inequality meets different preferences the outcomes of household decision making can only be predicted when the structural inequality and the individual preferences are known. In the chapter on fertility preferences, I examine this issue within the framework of intrahousehold bargaining models while considering in more detail how inequality of control over resources affects household decision making. Controlling for further exogenous effects, I find that women's bargaining power decreases the number of children while men's bargaining power significantly increases it.

Just as with gender inequality, differing preferences have welfare implications for the individual, but also for the household as a whole. If the nutritional status of children improves faster with women's income compared to men's income, these implications become immediately obvious (Hoddinott and Haddad 1995, Thomas 1994). Identifying and understanding the process of household decision making as well as determining the wants and goals of women and men can contribute to the formulation and improvement of policies. For example, women, as the ones who prefer less children, might be easier to address in the course of family planning programs as compared to men. However, as the results on bargaining power and fertility show, such programs can only be successful if men are adequately involved in the family planning process. This is because due to their preference for a large family and given their often high bargaining power, men might successfully oppose any initiative taken by the woman to reduce the number of births. The PROGRESA program in Mexico, in which cash money transfers are given to mothers but *not* to fathers in exchange for sending children to school, is an example where the explicit consideration of preferences in political programs has the desired effect which is increasing school enrollment and performance (Behrman, Sengupta and Todd 2005).

Gender research involves a high level of complexity—even the identification of inequality and of preferences can pose difficult problems that, if not appropriately addressed, may lead to biased results and wrong conclusions. Part of the problem is that behavior depends on the surrounding environment, implying that if the environment changes, behavior or preferences may change as well. For example, the lacking response of farmers in developing countries to price increases of cash crops has been explained by missing markets for food, from which farm households could satisfy their own consumption needs (Marcel Fafchamps and Sadoulet 1991). The availability of such markets therefore determines production choices of farmers, which are thus state dependent: state 1 in which food markets are available and state 2, where no markets for food exist. Such considerations may hold for gender inequality as well. Under circumstances that favor gender equality, behavioral outcomes may be quite different as when inequality prevails.

The state dependency of behavior may render the identification of the presence of discrimination difficult. In the analysis of production, the existence of gender inequality regarding access to productive resources as land or credit is often implicitly assumed and hence the sometimes observed lower productivity of female headed households (FHH) in agricultural production is associated with inequality. However, in the second chapter I present an example where the negative effects from tenure insecurity become only obvious when women farmers are not at risk to fall short of income (which would imply falling (deeper) into poverty). In cases where this risk is high FHH supply more labor thus increasing production outcomes despite tenure insecurity. Furthermore, these effects are only apparent, when explicitly considering the different institutional constraints that limit women's farm decision making. There is thus a state dependency, where the state is associated with the income risk being perceived by the farmer as well as with the current institutional setting. The interpretation that women are not affected by structural inequality because one does not observe its negative impact can therefore be false if other factors overcompensate these effects. In order to correctly identify relationships between inequality and outcomes, it is crucial to take into account state dependencies and explicitly considering them in the analysis of gender inequality.

The state dependency of behavior applies to the analysis of differing preferences, too. The preference structures of women and men can be directly observed through individual consumption behavior. In the case of fertility goals, data on desired family size of men and women can be compared in order to detect differences across gender. However, there are examples where structural inequality may determine preferences as examined in chapter 4. If women's access to means of old age security is limited, women may have an interest to 'invest' in their children in terms of health and education in order to enable them to care for their mother during old age. If this holds true, then preferences are state dependent and might change with improved access to markets for old age security.

The conclusion that women unambiguously spend more on food might therefore be too general and neglects the underlying state dependency. In response to a regime switch, e.g., the introduction of a public insurance scheme, women may change their behavior. If it turns out that preferences are state dependent and determined by prevailing circumstances, then policies designed for a certain context may fail if applied to another. Analyzing preferences without considering the associated structural inequality that may have generated these preferences thus can lead to wrong conclusions in scientific and policy terms. As yet, only few studies in economics (see Haddad (1999) for an exploration of that topic) have investigated the underlying causes of differing preferences among gender. Part of the goal of this study is to fill this gap.

Different preference structures have further implications for the measurement of welfare. In order to compare levels of income across households, economists commonly resort to the concept of equivalence scales which summarize the demographic profile—usually size and composition—of a household. Such scales are used to deflate household income to render it comparable to the income of a benchmark household. In practice, equivalence scales are estimated using household demand data. However, given that household demand is driven by preferences, the estimation of equivalence scales may thus be severely biased if preferences systematically differ across gender (or any other individual characteristic). As will be shown in chapter 4, such gender differences are most obvious regarding spending on food but hold also for other goods as tobacco or alcohol. The subsequent analysis in chapter 5 demonstrates that it is therefore questionable whether equivalence scales can be meaningfully estimated at all. If the measurement of welfare is dependent on preferences it must be biased as soon as preferences differ according to characteristics like the sex of the head of household.

Gender inequality still prevails in many parts of African society and it is evident that in present day Africa the women's set of constraints is often more restrictive as compared to that of men. In the agricultural context, these constraints are manifested by the agricultural production system that characterizes many regions in sub-Saharan Africa. In this system women and men cultivate different plots of land on their own account. The prevailing duality of the legal system further contributes to these constraints as customary law often systematically disadvantages women regarding their control rights over land. Lacking the right to possess land often inhibits women from obtaining credits, since formal credit institutions usually require a collateral (Migot-Adholla et al. 1991). Given the constraints women are facing in accessing land, obtaining a credit, starting a business, discriminatory wage regimes, etc., one needs to be concerned about the high numbers of female headed households and its implication for development. The incidence of women heading a household is in Africa exceptionally high and often amounts to more than 30 percent (Schäfer 2002). These features render Africa a continent where gender research is particularly crucial to enable the formulation of policies that aim to improve equitable and sustainable opportunities across gender. The aim of this study is thus to contribute to this question. Though the main focus is on Eastern Africa, many of the results can be generalized to the context of other regions as well.

# 2 One size fits all? Female headed households and access to resources in Kenya

## 2.1 Introduction

Studies considered with productivity in female (FHH) and male headed households (MHH) find that FHH appear to be either less, equally, or even more productive compared to MHH. Lower productivity of FHH has been reported by Bindlish, Evenson and Gbetibouo (1993), Chipande (1987), Dalton, Masters and Foster (1997), and Evenson and Mwabu (1998), which is often explained by women's insecure land rights (see also Doss 2001, Doss and Morris 2001). If land rights are insecure or women lack the power to make on-farm investment decisions, investments into land improvement and productivity increasing technologies are not undertaken, implying that production remains below the possibility frontier (Chipande 1987, Saito and Weidemann 1990, Saito, Mekonnen and Spurling 1994). Soil conservation or the cultivation of cash crops such as cotton are examples for labor intensive technologies which potentially increase productivity in the long run, but where tenure insecurity leads to non-adoption (see Anim 1999, Chipande 1987, Barbier 1998, Forson 1999, Lapar and Pandey 1999, Pender and Kerr 1998, Shively 1997).

Despite the often reproduced result of low productivity of FHH, other studies report mixed results. In their investigation of improved crop variety adoption, Doss and Morris (2001) find that the adoption rate of hybrid maize is equal among FHH and MHH in Ghana. However, FHH were less likely to adopt modern varieties of other crops. Analyzing data from Benin and Malawi, Minot, Kherallah and Berry (2000) find that FHH in Malawi are more likely to use fertilizer than MHH. For the case of Benin, there are no significant differences. In other instances, studies report that FHH achieve the same yield per hectare or produce even more than MHH (Bindlish and Evenson 1993, Moock 1976). In sum, it seems impossible to make *a priori* predictions on the productivity of FHH since they turn out to be less, equally or more productive compared with MHH.

This paper is an attempt to reconcile these findings by constructing a model that accounts for productivity effects which arise from tenure insecurity and the risk of falling short of income. Both affect productivity through the supply of labor, but they do so in opposite directions. While tenure insecurity tends to decrease labor effort, income risks increase it as subsistence farmers want to avoid falling (deeper) into poverty. Depending on which of these risks prevails in the perception of farmers, they become either more or less productive than a benchmark farmer who faces none of these constraints.[1]

---

[1] It should be noted that the concept of productivity used here does not imply that farmers in rural areas of developing countries do produce on a large scale. The produced output is often only slightly above the poverty line and being (relatively) productive often implies to produce a little more than in an

A common prediction on how risk averse farmers respond to tenure uncertainty, is that they reduce effort and investment, i.e. they produce less output as compared to a risk neutral farmer (Feder, Just and Zilberman 1988, Besley 1995). A theoretical justification can be found in Sandmo (1971) who introduced price uncertainty into the profit maximization problem of a competitive firm. A major result of his study is that firms respond to uncertainty by reducing inputs and consequently produce less output. However, the theory has serious shortcomings when applied to the context of subsistence farming, where part of the output is consumed by the producers. Subsistence farmers cannot afford to reduce effort since lower output implies that they would fall into even deeper poverty. Early concerns about the applicability of Sandmo's model to subsistence farming are stated by Finkelshtain and Chalfant (1991) who theoretically demonstrate that depending on the share of home consumption and the income elasticity of household demand for the subsistence good, farmers may well produce more when exposed to income risk. They also find that the common Arrow-Pratt measure of risk aversion falls short in measuring the true risk aversion of subsistence farmers.

The model developed in this paper as well as the subsequent empirical analysis establish that how farmers respond to the risk associated with tenure insecurity depends on the availability of alternative income options which guarantee a certain level of income. A major finding presented here is that farmers switch between two different states which are determined by the probability of falling short of income. If this risk is high, farmers cannot afford to adjust their production to other risks like tenure insecurity as they otherwise would be even poorer. On the other hand, when the risk to fall into poverty is low, farmers respond to tenure insecurity by reducing production. This they do at an increasing rate, the farer they get ahead from their subjective poverty line.[2] The mixed results concerning the productivity of FHH in comparison to MHH may therefore be explained by their different exposures to income risk.

Studies concerned with comparisons of agricultural production between FHH and MHH usually neglect the fact that the concept of a FHH is multifaceted and not easily subsumed under a single heading. FHH may be distinguished according to a number of criteria as for example the marital status of the head of household, whether a woman is the household decision maker or the main income earner, etc. By applying these criteria, different implications arise for the welfare of the different categories of FHH (Drèze and Srinivasan 1997, Fuwa 2000, Kennedy and Peters 1992, Rosenhouse 1989). Furthermore, in some regions marital status, demographic characteristics and the position of a woman as being the main household decision maker determine the security of land rights, implying that each type

---

environment that does not impose any risks on the farmer.

[2]The risk of falling short of income is at least partly a subjective risk as it depends on the personal perception of being poor or not. This is the reason why I am not referring to an explicit poverty line in the empirical section.

of FHH should exhibit different patterns of production.
Tenure insecurity is not the only risk that women as heads of household are facing. Outmigrating husbands often leave the household and literally take the farm decision power with them, such that women are not allowed to do any on-farm investment decisions or crop choices. In what follows, I treat tenure insecurity and low levels of decision making competence interchangeably as they lead to the same conclusion regarding the incentive structure to invest in productivity increases.

Although the welfare implications arising from different forms of FHH have been investigated, as yet no study was done on the production side of FHH in smallholder farming in sub-Saharan Africa. Using a large scale household survey from Kenya which provides detailed information on household characteristics and farming, I distinguish eight different categories of FHH, each of which associated with a different scheme of incentives to invest into farming and investigate whether these household categories are sufficiently different to exhibit household specific patterns of production arising from different sets of constraints these households are subjected to.

## 2.2 The problem of classifying FHH

The most common way to classify FHH is self-reported headship which is a standard question in most household surveys. Usage of this indicator in empirical studies is based on the assumption that FHH are a homogeneous group, thus ignoring that there are many ways out of which a FHH can emerge and according to which FHH can be categorized. One possible further classification is marital status, which includes marriage, widowhood, or divorced women. Another category may be demographic characteristics of the household. A significant number of FHH result from temporary outmigration of the husband, seeking employment in urban areas. Another example is polygamy which is still a wide spread pattern of family organization in sub-Saharan Africa. Polygamous households are often part of a larger household compound which is not necessarily captured by household surveys. Such a household may be identified as a FHH, although it belongs to an array of different but related household units where usually a man is responsible for household decisions. It is likely that such households operate under entirely different conditions as compared to widows or unmarried women.

These criteria, though important means to identify different categories of FHH, do not comprise further interesting cases. Many FHH are characterized by the fact that men are entirely or in part responsible for on-farm decision making while in other cases women are the sole decision makers. Kennedy and Peters (1992) have classified these groups as *de facto* and *de jure* FHH, where only in the latter the woman is considered to be the legal and customary household decision maker. A *de facto* FHH on the other hand is characterized by a married woman whose husband is absent most of the time. Women in these households are not necessarily the principal household decision maker.

Before classifying FHH, it is necessary to ask for the specific constraints that women face. Women in many sub-Saharan African countries are disadvantaged in terms of access to land, which translates into difficulties to obtain credits and therefore agricultural inputs (see Gopal and Salim (1998) for an extensive review of women and land rights in Eastern Africa). In some cases, women are not allowed to register land in their names and are thus dependent on a male relative, be it their husband, father, brother, son, etc., who can hold a title for them. Even where legal reforms have brought about the right for women to possess land as in Kenya, men often registered all household land in their names, even if it customarily belonged to the woman. If the owner of the land title dies or separates, the woman may lose access rights to land as the titles are often passed to a male member of the family.

Land that is not entitled in the farmer's name cannot be used as collateral for obtaining credits, which inhibits the adoption of improved crop varieties and complementary inputs. Lack of collateral has been found to be a major reason why women tend to be excluded from credit programs (Saito et al. 1994). Failure to adopt modern technologies would therefore arise not necessarily due to a generally imperfect input market, but as a consequence of characteristics inherent to the social status of women farmers. But there are further issues that disadvantage women. Doss (2001) and Doss and Morris (2001) report that male extension workers are reluctant to visit women such that women are further constrained in obtaining information. Finally, men may be important for establishing business contacts and are often responsible for marketing cash crops. In rural Kenya, men often serve as middlemen between women and the market for capital goods and agricultural inputs (Savane 1986).

Whether a woman as head of household faces such constraints depends on the way out of which female headship has emerged. The death of the husband is an exogenous shock that immediately changes the woman's economic and social status. Such shock may imply that access to land becomes insecure. This holds also for the case of Kenya where, although land is legally a private property that can be sold, the major means to access land is through the family. Among the Kikuyu, who constitute the largest ethnic group in Kenya, land is alloted along patrilineages, where the 'guardian' of the lineage assigns land to the sons. This is mostly done upon marriage, but can also happen before. The married son who receives the land is obliged to give a certain share of the land to his wife such that marriage guarantees access to land for women. Therefore, within marriage, women have relatively secure land rights. However, she cannot sell any land received from the family. Women are also excluded from inheriting land. Even though the Kenyan law has by now legalized the bequest of land to daughters, most family elders continue to give the land exclusively to sons (Davison 1988).

Under the British colonial rule, land entitlements have been introduced in the course of the Swynnerton Plan that came into law in 1954. The major aim of the plan was to reform land ownership system by introducing a formal land entitlement system that induces agricultural development through setting proper incentives.[3] A result of this effort was that many men took the chance to register all family land in their names. Even though, their wives were formerly granted land for cultivation, women had no possibility to claim that land legally.

As noted, within marriage, women's access to land is secure and land cannot be taken away by the husband. The woman also often exercises the right to control the produce of the land and to decide what to crop and what to sell. Hence, as long as the conjugal arrangement holds, land rights are well defined, but if marriage ends, the woman's access to land is at risk. In case of separation or death of the husband, the family of the husband often claims back the land which they have initially given to their son. This may even happen years after the passing of the man, in case he had a younger brother and the parents become in need to give out land. However, if the woman happens to become a widow, often a brother of the deceased husband takes over farm decision making. 'Formally', the husband's family therefore still holds the land rights, but for the widow this implies that she is granted a means of survival, for the brother as the 'representative' decision maker guarantees that she can keep the land (Davison 1988).

In some other cases, the widow or separated woman may cultivate the land on behalf of one of her sons or brothers, which puts her into the same position as when a relative of the passed husband took over decision making power. Unmarried women may receive land from their father which enables these women to form an independent household. However, these women may not have control rights over the land because the father often keeps control such that in case one of his sons marries, he still has land at his disposal to give to his son (Davison 1988, Yngstrom 2002). Men on the other hand do not face such difficulties as tenure insecurity as they are favored through the traditional land distribution system.

Although the examples bear some specificity for Kenya, it is easy to find examples from other ethnic groups other than the Kikuyu either in Kenya or other Eastern African countries where mechanisms of land allotment and marriage are very similar (for further examples and references see Davison 1988, Gopal and Salim 1998, Yngstrom 2002). The constraints of widows bear similarity to those women left by their husbands (Gopal and Salim 1998). However, women may also seek divorce. This decision may be driven by the consideration that she can achieve a higher level of welfare outside marriage. Using data from Jamaica, Handa (1996b) finds that some women gain more from staying unmarried since they have independent access to resources. Regarding divorce, women may seek

---

[3]Although the Swynnerton plan was launched in 1954, its implementation is still ongoing as a lot of land has not yet been registered.

separation only when having secure access to land and exerting full decision making power.

Another widespread phenomenon is the temporary out-migration of husbands seeking employment in urban areas. In Uganda it has been found that husbands—although absent—maintain the decision making power even when they are away from home over extended periods.[4] Asked why they did not apply improved farming technologies, the women responded that they do not have the right to make decisions about investments (see also Kennedy and Peters 1992). In these households, men often still play a dominant role in household decision making while the woman is not allowed to decide about important on-farm investments.

The examples cited provide a guideline for constructing different classes of FHH according to their marital status and the presence of a man who affects household decisions and determines tenure security. A widow who receives support from her sons is not exposed to the same constraints as a widow who needs to argue with her husband's family about the land. A FHH which emerged out of temporary outmigration is cropping under different constraints when the man still keeps the right for on-farm decision making compared to a fully responsible woman. All these different situations imply different constraints which affect agricultural production and thus lead to varying levels of productivity. The model developed in the next section aims to account for the heterogeneity of FHH while explaining the observed ambiguity of productivity levels of FHH.

## 2.3 The model

In order to derive the conditions under which FHH exhibit either higher, equal, or lower levels of productivity compared with MHH, I construct a household optimization model that allows for investigating labor supply decisions under two different states. The one state is achieved when the household's income is above the subjective poverty line. In this case, the standard model as the one by Sandmo predicts that risk averse farmers would reduce labor supply when exposed to tenure uncertainty. On the other hand, in the second state, farmers face the risk of falling below the poverty line that changes their response to tenure uncertainty. Reducing effort is not an option as it would imply becoming even poorer and more deprived. In order to escape that trap, farmers need to increase effort to avoid becoming poorer. A major result of the model developed below is therefore that tenure insecurity does not necessarily lead to a reduction of labor supply, depending on which perception of risk prevails: (i) tenure uncertainty or (ii) the risk of falling short of income. The model is kept simple and considers only labor as an essential variable input. However, the model is generalizable to all other inputs such as fertilizer, pesticides or draft power as well. Land, the second important

---
[4]I am thankful to John Pender for pointing this out to me.

input, is considered fixed throughout the following analysis.

I begin with a simple framework in which utility is maximized under perfect security, which will be extended later in the text. The farmer is endowed with a fixed amount of labor time $T$ which she allocates across two different income generating activities: crop cultivation and off-farm work. If the farmer has the opportunity to generate off-farm income she receives a wage rate $w$ so that her off-farm income will be $wl$, where $l$ denotes her off-farm labor supply. This activity does not need to be restricted to denote only wage labor, but $w$ may also represent marginal returns to off-farm enterprises. Land $A$ is cultivated using labor $T - l$ which gives rise to a production function of the form $q = f(T - l, A)$ for which it is assumed that $f' > 0$ and $f'' < 0$, where $f'$ and $f''$ denote the first and second derivative of $f$ with respect to $l$. Each activity of the woman involves a cost which is captured by a function $c_w$ and $c_f$ respectively, which share the usual properties of a cost function, that is $c' > 0$ and $c'' > 0$. The costs arise from the disutility of labor. Alternatively, one may think of more sophisticated representations where the costs in $c_w$ arise from purchasing inputs for off-farm enterprises, from searching for a job, transportation, etc. Equivalently, one may extend $c_f$ to include the needs to purchase seeds, fertilizer or pesticides without substantial complication and without changing the basic results. However, for reasons of simplicity I focus on labor supply only and thus the only variable driving the cost function is $l$. Combining the productive activities with the cost functions, the woman faces an income given by

$$y = wl - c_w(l) + f(T - l, A) - c_f(T - l) \qquad (1)$$

This equation describes the situation of a farmer who does not encounter any constraints other than her disutility and restrictions implied by wage rates and the technology applied. To capture tenure insecurity, let $\pi(\theta)$ be the probability that the farmer can retain the benefits from labor supply (or investments) in future periods. From $\pi$, we obtain expected returns from farming by

$$E(f(T - l, A)) = \pi(\theta) \cdot f(T - l, A) + (1 - \pi(\theta)) \cdot 0 \qquad (2)$$

The probability $\pi$ or the level of tenure security depends on the woman's level of bargaining power as she needs to defend her land against the claims of her husband's family. It is convenient for the subsequent analysis to assume that the bargaining power parameter $\theta$ directly translates into $\pi$ such that $\theta = \pi$. If the woman has the means to defend the land against claims of her husband's family, that is, if $\theta$ is equal to or close to 1, then she faces a high level of tenure security. Note that in the present framework $\pi$ does not necessarily need to represent tenure security, but may equally denote the power to make on-farm investment decisions in case of absent husbands. In this regard, $\theta$ can also be interpreted as the power to exert the right to decide.

The second modification concerns the probability that households only achieve a level of income below the poverty line. Very poor households need to define an income target that ensures a minimum welfare level, such as the satisfaction of a minimum level of nutrition, basic needs, etc. This income target is somewhat different from the usual notion of an income target that implies a backward bending labor supply curve where the target works as a threshold. In target income models, workers do not want to supply more labor, but value leisure higher than additional income, once the threshold has been achieved.[5] In the present setting, target income rather refers to a different concept, that is, farmers facing the risk of not achieving their minimum acceptable income, supply more labor in order to get as close as possible to the income target. Hence, households at risk of falling below their income target cannot afford to work less and thus exhibit a different cost function as compared to a wealthy household. Let the probability that a woman achieves her target be given by

$$p = \frac{1}{F(P) - F(0)} \int_0^P f(y) dy \qquad (3)$$

where $P$ is the target minimum acceptable income (for convenience one may think of $P$ as the (subjective) poverty line), $F(\cdot)$ is a cumulative distribution function, $f(\cdot)$ is the associated probability density, and $y$ is income.[6] Since $y$ is a function of available land size $A$, returns from market labor $w$, total availability of labor time $T$, but also of bargaining power $\theta$, we can write $p$ equivalently as $p(A, w, T, \theta)$. $p$ is the realization of a cumulative distribution function and is assumed to be increasing in all of its arguments. For instance, with rising wage rates, income increases as well as more labor is allocated to off-farm activities, which in turn increases the probability to achieve the income target. In the model below, the variable $p$ affects the shape of the cost functions which flatten when $p$ approaches zero.

Combining tenure insecurity and the probability to achieve the income target with (1) we get the program of the FHH

$$\max_y \; u(y)$$
$$\text{s.t.} \quad y = wl - pc_w(l) + \theta f(T - l, A) - pc_f(T - l) \qquad (4)$$

Maximization of (4) with respect to $l$ generates the conditions for optimal labor allocation across the two activities

$$w = pc'_w + [\theta f' - pc'_f] \qquad (5)$$

---
[5]See Camerer, Babcock, Loewenstein and Thaler (1997) and Farber (2005) for investigations on target incomes and labor supply.

[6]Note, that this expression is derived from a truncated density function which is truncated at $P$.

Women allocate labor such that the going market wage rate equals the marginal cost of working plus the difference between marginal returns from labor and the marginal costs from farming. After solving for $l$, optimal labor supply can be expressed as a function of $\theta$ and $p$, as well as of $A$ and $w$. Denote optimal labor supply as $l^*(\theta, p, A, w)$. Applying the envelope theorem with respect to $\theta$ gives

$$\frac{\partial l^*}{\partial \theta} = \frac{f' - p'c'_f + p'c'_w}{\theta f'' - pc''_f - pc''_w} \qquad (6)$$

The numerator of the right hand side is positive as it is a scaled version of the right and side of (5) which is positive, since $0 \leq p' \leq 1$. The denominator is negative, because $f'' < 0$, $c''_f, c''_w > 0$. Thus we have

$$\frac{\partial l^*}{\partial \theta} < 0 \qquad (7)$$

Since $l^*$ represents optimal off-farm labor supply, a negative sign of (7) implies that FHH increase farm labor once the level of tenure security improves. The results demonstrate that land is underutilized as long as income from farming is insecure. This effect is illustrated in figure 1. The upper solid concave line denotes production where $\theta = 1$ and full tenure security is achieved. The disutility or cost function is given by the lower convex curve. Labor is allocated until the farmer's marginal productivity, depicted by the tangent on the production curve, equals her marginal costs, depicted by the tangent on the cost curve, such that optimal labor supply amounts to $l_n$ which translates into production outcome $q_n$. If tenure is insecure, that is, when $\theta < 1$, expected output decreases while generating a new production frontier which is illustrated by the lower dashed concave curve. As a response to lower expected returns, the woman adjusts her optimal labor supply until the two tangents representing marginal productivity and marginal cost are just parallel. Thus she reduces effort from $l_n$ to $l_\theta$ in order to equate marginal cost and the marginal productivity arising from the lower expected returns. This reduction of effort results in an accompanying decrease of output from $q$ to $q_\theta$ which establishes the result that with $\theta < 1$ outputs decrease.

A similar effect running from $p$ to labor allocation and production outcomes, but with the contrary implication, is shown in figure 2. Here the upper solid convex curve depicts a cost function that represents the case where the farmer faces no risk of falling short of income. Thus, she can equate her marginal productivity to her marginal disutility of labor which implies labor supply $l_n$ which leads to production outcome $q_n$ just as in the previous graph. Now assume the household faces an income risk through decreasing off-farm incomes which is expressed by values of $p < 1$. In this case, $p$ depresses the cost curve downwards as is exemplified by the lower dashed curve. In adjusting to this income risk farmers equate their marginal productivity to the marginal cost of the new disutility function implying that in optimum costs shift from $c_n$ to $c_p$ where costs are given by

Figure 1: Effects of $\theta$ on labor allocation

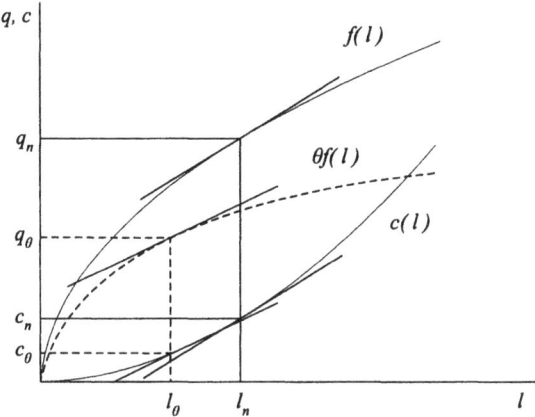

the vertical axis. In the new equilibrium the household supplies $l_p$ units of labor and achieves output $q_p$. Hence, if tenure is secure and only $p$ varies, then farm labor supply and consequently production outcomes increase with decreasing $p$.

The comparative statics regarding the change of the return from off-farm employment yield

$$\frac{\partial l^*}{\partial w} = \frac{1 + p'c'_f - p'c'_w}{pc''_w + pc''_f - \theta f''} \quad (8)$$

Expression (8) is positive as long as the marginal disutility of labor in farming $c'_f$ is larger than the marginal disutility from working on the labor market $c'_w$. This holds when labor markets are underdeveloped or wage rates are low, which are the cases I am focusing on. A positive sign of $\frac{\partial l^*}{\partial w}$ implies that labor is withdrawn from agriculture and allocated to off-farm activities if the wage rate is rising. With no other options but farming available, households would employ all labor in agriculture yielding the first order conditions

$$\theta f' = pc'_f \quad (9)$$

In order to analyze the impact of $p$ and $\theta$ on farming efficiency, I focus on farming only and investigate the effects of farm labor supply in response to varying $\theta$ and $p$ while holding all other factors fixed. To facilitate the exposition, I focus on equation 9 and neglect for simplicity the existence of labor markets. It should be noted that the general result is not affected by this simplification. However, later I introduce off-farm activities through investigating the effect of variations

**Figure 2: Effects of $p$ on labor allocation**

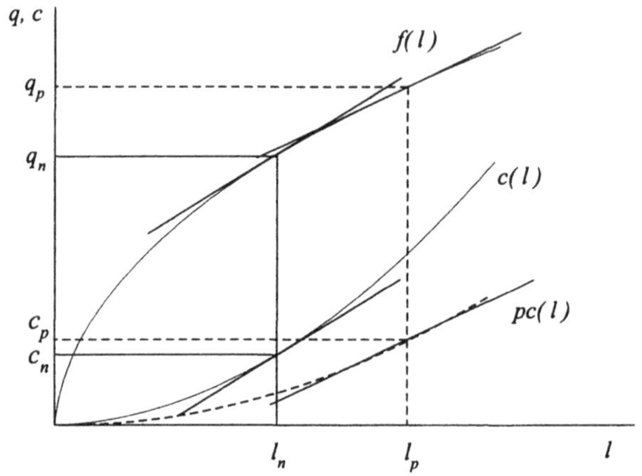

of the wage rate $w$ on $p$. The crucial assumption is that $p$ increases with $w$, which implies that households reallocate more and more labor towards the generation of income from off-farm activities—a result revealed by equation (8). To see how labor allocation and productivity is determined, I consider four cases summarized in table 1.

In case 1, the woman has achieved full tenure security and achieves target income with probability 1. That is, wage rates or land size are large enough to ensure that $p = 1$. In this case, household production is only constrained by personal disutility of labor and the household achieves average levels of productivity. Case 2 refers to women for whom tenure is insecure, implying that labor supply is below average. The FHH allocates labor such that the marginal productivity

**Table 1: Different cases with missing labor markets**

| Case 1 | $f' = c'_f$ | $\theta = 1;\ p = 1$ | Average efficiency |
|---|---|---|---|
| Case 2 | $\theta f' = c'_f$ | $\theta < 1;\ p = 1$ | Below average efficiency |
| Case 3 | $f' = pc'_f$ | $\theta = 1;\ p < 1$ | Above average efficiency |
| Case 4 | $\theta f' = pc'_f$ | $\theta < 1;\ p < 1$ | Indeterminate |

of farming equals the marginal cost. But since $\theta < 1$, the expected marginal returns are lower compared to case 1 households, implying that marginal costs must be lower as well. Consequently case 2 households exhibit a lower supply of labor and therefore lower output. In case 3, the curvature of the cost function is flattened through the impact of the low probability to achieve the income target. Hence, labor supply must be above average and, given land and labor time $T$, the household produces more than a case 1 household. Finally, in case 4 both factors, tenure insecurity and low probability to achieve target income, affect labor supply decisions. The location of these households relative to the efficiency frontier depends on the curvature of the production and cost functions which is determined by $\theta$ and $p$. This implies that empirically this case cannot be distinguished from the other three cases when only production output is observed. Given the shape of the two functions, labor supply might be above, below or even exactly equal to case 1 households. Optimal labor supply is somewhere between $l_\theta$ and $l_p$ as exemplified in figures 1 and 2. An appealing feature of the model as summarized by the four cases is that it allows for explaining different levels of productivity even in the absence of labor markets.

The four cases in table 1 further imply another result: with increasing $w$, $p$ increases as well and the impact of tenure insecurity in case 4 becomes stronger. To see this, consider the production outcome $q_m$, which is the level of production of a case 4 household and define the production outcomes $q_u$ and $q_l$ for case 2 and case 3 as upper and lower bounds respectively. Since in households for which case 4 applies $\theta < 1$ and $p < 1$ the household's production outcome $q_m$ is located somewhere between $q_u$ and $q_l$. But with increasing $p$, the case 4 household approaches and eventually transforms into a case 2 household. Consequently, $q_m$ approaches $q_u$ which is associated with case 2 households; household production declines. The opposite case can be constructed when $p$ is kept fixed and one allows $\theta$ to increase.

The model shows that the farmer's response to tenure insecurity is state dependent. When the farmer faces the risk of an income shortfall, the effect of tenure insecurity is overcompensated by the effect of $p$ and output may not be decreased at all or may even be higher as in households exhibiting the same levels of $\theta$ but large values of $p$. For relatively wealthier farmers, there is only a small risk of becoming poorer, which why tenure insecurity exerts its full effect in decreasing production. That is, with given bargaining power $\theta$ and given probability $p$ to achieve target income, FHH are either more, equally or less efficient compared to a MHH.[7] Using the model it is possible to explain the seemingly contradicting findings from the various empirical studies that have been concerned with agri-

---

[7]In principal it is possible that a MHH correspond to a case 1 or case 3 household. However, it is assumed that there is no characteristic other than low off-farm incomes that is systematically related to case 3. So, when joining all MHH within a single category, MHH must be on average more productive compared to a FHH to which case 3 applies.

cultural production and the comparison of FHH and MHH. These findings have implications for empirical studies as well: the different states can only be identified when the levels of $\theta$ and $p$ are appropriately controlled for.

## 2.4 The data

The data used in this study stems from the Kenyan Welfare Monitoring Survey III, which has been conducted during 1997 and covers more than 11,000 households. However, due to a large number of missing responses on agricultural inputs and urban households not engaged in agriculture, the total sample size reduces to 4,088 observations. The FHH indicator builds on self-reported headship to achieve comparability with other studies. The data allows for distinguishing different categories of FHH according to the three criteria (i) marital status, (ii) demographic characteristics and (iii) main household decision maker. Marital status, which is a standard question in most large scale household surveys, is probably the most obvious feature to categorize FHH. The questionnaire includes the categories married, never married, widowed, divorced or separated, and whether the household is part of a polygamous household compound. In almost all households of the married category, no husband is currently staying at home and thus these are named henceforth *Temporary*. A second category covered by the data is whether the woman is divorced or separated. For this category it would be desirable to know who initiated the separation as it may affect the results, since women who seek divorce may be well prepared to live outside the household (e.g. through land ownership, wage employment, etc.). Women who have been left by their partners might be in a much less favorable situation (Gopal and Salim 1998). Divorced women are termed *Divorced*. The next category are widows who are named accordingly. Women who have never been married are called *Single* and finally women from polygamous households are classified *Polygamous*. It would be desirable to distinguish single women according to their choice of being unmarried, that is, whether land endowment has influenced the choice not to marry. Although, of the single women in the sample, only four indicate that a male non-relative resides permanently in the household, this does not imply that these women do not have a male partner. The partner may just not live with the woman in the same household.

The final characteristic used for classifying FHH refers to the main household decision maker, which determines the categories *de jure* and *de facto* FHH, whereas in the former category, women are considered as having control over household decisions while the *de facto* category denotes FHH in which not the woman does on-farm decisions but a male relative. The questionnaire contains a question on who decides on farm investments. The answer is taken here as an indication of the true head of household: FHH where the woman is responsible for farm investments are allocated into the *de jure* category and classified as *de facto* otherwise. Note, that these categories do not immediately imply the status of bargaining power, which is determined only in combination with marital status. In total, eight different categories emerge from applying these categories to the data. The different classes mainly arise from distinguishing the marital status with respect to *de jure* or *de facto* FHH. To facilitate exposition the categories are abbreviated *DJ* and *DF* respectively.[8] Only unmarried and polygamous households are treated as special cases and are not further categorized according to the decision maker.

The meaning of the terms *de jure* and *de facto* FHH as applied in this study does not entirely correspond to its common use (see Kennedy and Peters (1992) for an early application). The category *de jure* is usually used to classify widows, divorced and separated, as well as single FHH, while *de facto* refers to households where the woman is married but her husband is mostly not present. However, the terms are used here to further distinguish these FHH categories, as the sole application of the *de jure* and *de facto* categories fall short of fully capturing the true household decision maker.

Finally, it is necessary to analyze the levels of bargaining power of the women from the respective household categories. As in the previous section, the term bargaining power is only used for brevity and should not be taken literally, as *DF Temporary* are not threatened to lose their land, but are characterized by low levels of decision making power. Since the absent husbands still aim to control farm investments, these households are characterized by low levels of bargaining power. *DJ Temporary* households on the opposite fully control farm investments and hence exhibit high levels of $\theta$. Among widows, those with male support, that is, where a male relative has the principal right to decide on farm investments, have a better bargaining position than their counterparts, where the woman is fully on her own. Thus, *DF Widows* have high levels of bargaining power while *DJ Widows* are at permanent risk that the husband's family claims back the land. Table 2 gives an overview to the bargaining power position of the different household categories. The question marks in the table indicate that levels of bargaining power and hence that of efficiency cannot be unambiguously determined *a priori*.

Table 3 shows the different classifications in terms of absolute numbers and shares of the sample. The share of FHH amounts to 34.4 % of the total sample. Widows add up to the largest category and account for 49.1% of all FHH, while 32.7% are *Temporary* FHH. The large share of *DJ Temporary* indicates that labor migration is a frequent cause for the emergence of FHH in general. The other household categories, *Divorced*, *Single*, and *Polygamous* are relatively small and

---

[8]There are 28 households in the *DF Temporary* category who indicate that a husband is present. This seems to be unusual and may be the result of misreporting. Excluding these household leaves the results unchanged. When forming an extra category of these households, the new category exhibits the same signs and levels of significance as the *DF Temporary* category. I therefore decided to keep these households as *DF Temporary*.

Table 2: Different classes of FHH and their associated levels of bargaining power

| FHH categories | Situation | Who decides? | Bargaining power |
|---|---|---|---|
| DJ Temporary | Outmigrated husband | Wife | High |
| DF Temporary | Outmigrated husband | Husband | Low |
| DJ Widow | Deceased husband | Woman | Low |
| DF Widow | Deceased husband | Male relative | High |
| DJ Divorce | Marriage divorced or separated | Woman | ? |
| DF Divorce | Marriage divorced or separated | Male relative | ? |
| Single | Unmarried | Woman | ? |
| Polygamous | Polygamous | Woman or clan head | ? |

do not account for a large share of the total sample.

Columns 4 and 5 from table 3 report the average endowment with land and earned income per capita. The comparison of MHH and FHH does not reveal substantial differences regarding the distribution of land. However, when looking at the disaggregated FHH indicators some differences become apparent. All *DF* households have on average one hectare more land compared to their *DJ* counterparts. Only *DF Divorce* households have less land than the *DJ Divorce* households. Polygamous households have a land size which is above the sample average which might be due to counting all land that belongs to the compound. Regarding income, *DJ Widows* exhibit the lowest income per capita from resources other than farming, while *DF Temporary* generate the highest average income. At the time of the survey the poverty line was set at 1,297 Kenyan shillings, which is still higher than the reported average off-farm income for any of the household categories including MHH. Also, per capita income from farming is equally low. Such low incomes are reflected by the rate of poverty. It has been estimated that in 1997 about 46 percent of households in rural areas are below the food poverty line.

## 2.5 Empirical implementation

### 2.5.1 Constructing a test for the relevance of the four cases for the different FHH categories

The goal of the empirical analysis is to detect different levels of productivity among FHH which point to different exposure to tenure insecurity and low levels of decision making power. I first estimate the efficiency frontier using a variable cost function and in a second step investigate whether deviations from the frontier are systematically related to different kinds of FHH. Tenure insecurity is determined by the household's level of bargaining power, which is shown for each household type in table 4 where the first column is repeated from table 2 to facilitate the exposition of the empirical strategy. To determine where households are

Table 3: Shares of FHH categories and resource endowment

| | Total | Share (in %) of total | Share (in %) of FHH | Land† (in hectare) | Off-farm inc.† (in Kenyan shillings) | Farm inc.† (in Kenyan shillings) |
|---|---|---|---|---|---|---|
| MHH | 2680 | 65.56 | | 3.0 | 465.00 | 1093.75 |
| FHH | 1408 | 34.44 | | 3.0 | 333.33 | 807.78 |
| DF Temporary | 143 | 3.50 | 10.16 | 2.0 | 300.00 | 914.36 |
| DJ Temporary | 317 | 7.75 | 22.51 | 3.0 | 800.00 | 744.00 |
| DF Widow | 291 | 7.12 | 20.67 | 2.0 | 250.00 | 1122.95 |
| DJ Widow | 400 | 9.78 | 28.41 | 3.0 | 366.67 | 618.14 |
| DF Divorce | 21 | 0.51 | 1.49 | 2.0 | 257.15 | 1395.67 |
| DJ Divorce | 63 | 1.54 | 4.47 | 1.5 | 568.7 | 963.33 |
| Single | 24 | 0.59 | 1.70 | 1.7 | 400.00 | 1806.80 |
| Polygamous | 149 | 3.64 | 10.58 | 3.5 | 375.00 | 797.88 |
| Total sample | 4088 | | | 3.0 | 400.00 | 933.33 |

†Medians reported.

located relative to the efficiency frontier, a dummy variable is introduced into the cost function that accounts for each FHH category. A significant dummy implies a shift of that household category either closer to or further away from the efficiency frontier as compared to the average MHH. Given the estimation approach employed and described below, a negative result implies higher efficiency scores while a positive parameter indicates that the respective household is less productive.

Furthermore, the empirical exercise aims to discover state dependent responses to insecurity. The fundamental result of the model is that tenure insecurity exerts a different effect in each regime with implications for labor supply and productivity. Also, for households with perfect security the different regimes have efficiency implications as is evident from cases 3 and 1. The regime is determined by $p$, which represents the risk of falling short of income. The level of $p$ is measured by the level of off-farm income generated by the respective household. The off-farm income is interacted with the dummy in order to determine the category specific effect. Its interpretation is simple: when the sign is significantly positive, then with increasing income the levels of farm inefficiency increase as well because households allocate more labor away from farming toward off-farm activities. This implies an undercultivation of the available land and thus increasing inefficiency.

To be able to interpret the results, it is necessary to clarify the possible assignment of households to the four cases. Column 3 of table 4 gives an account of which FHH category can be assigned to which case. The table further contains in column 4 and 5 the signs of the dummy variables that are conform to the predictions of the theory developed in the previous chapter. By the definition of the FHH categories, the only households facing low levels of $\theta$ are *DF Temporary* and *DJ Widow* households. This implies that these households can be assigned to either case 2 or case 4. Hence, based on the theory one would expect these two household categories to be more, equally or less efficient compared to MHH, when controlling for all other determinants of productivity. Which one of these three possibilities hold is an empirical question. When the sign is negative, the household belongs to case 4 because this is the only one of the two cases that allows above average levels of productivity (see table 1). When the coefficient is insignificant, the household may also be a case 4 household due to the same reason, as the effects from $\theta$ and $p$ may just neutralize each other.[9] When the sign of the dummy turns out to be significantly positive it is not possible to unambiguously assign the households to case 4 or case 2 as both cases allow for this option. However, as explained below, the information from the interaction term can be used to recover the case to which the household category belongs to.

*DJ Temporary* and *DF Widow* households are expected to be either equal to a case 1 or case 3 household as tenure insecurity does not affect them because of their high levels of bargaining power. The theory predicts that these households are either more or equally productive compared to average MHH, depending on the perception of income risk. Estimates of levels of productivity for this class of FHH are therefore predicted to be either negative or insignificant. A negative estimate means that these households are more productive than average MHH and thus are assigned to case 3. An insignificant parameter implies that there is no difference to the average MHH which is assumed to be equivalent to a case 1 household. Since it is unknown whether the remaining four FHH categories have on average a high or low value of $\theta$ no expectations can be formulated beforehand.

The theory further implies that households which are initially case 3 or case 4 households can transform into case 1 and case 2 households respectively. That is, with increasing off-farm income, $p$ is increasing and case 3 and 4 households eventually switch from one state into another. As laid out above, whether such transition exists is tested via the inclusion of an interaction term where off-farm income is interacted with each FHH category. Here again, the model implies some restrictions. Transiting from one state into another implies that households which have initially been a case 3 or case 4 household must become more inefficient with increasing incomes. That is, if a transition occurs, then the interaction term must be positive, meaning that when off-farm income activities become more attractive, more labor is allocated away from farming toward the off-farm income activity and levels of productivity decrease.

However, the theory offers even more restrictions: *DJ Temporary* and *DF Widow* can only exhibit a transition from case 3 to case 1 if case 3 households exist at all. This can easily be checked by referring to the dummy variable estimate of these households. If the dummy does not become significantly negative, there

---

[9] An insignificant parameter may also imply that neither tenure insecurity nor low levels of $p$ determine productive outcomes.

Table 4: Assignment of cases to FHH categories and expected signs of estimates

| FHH categories | Bargaining power | Possible cases | Possible sign of dummy | Possible sign of interaction term |
|---|---|---|---|---|
| DJ Temporary | High | 1,3 | 0,- | 0,+ |
| DF Temporary | Low | 2,4 | 0,-,+ | 0,+ |
| DJ Widow | Low | 2,4 | 0,-,+ | 0,+ |
| DF Widow | High | 1,3 | 0,- | 0,+ |
| DJ Divorce | ? | ? | ? | ? |
| DF Divorce | ? | ? | ? | ? |
| Single | ? | ? | ? | ? |
| Polygamous | ? | ? | ? | ? |

are no case 3 households and a transition cannot occur. For *DF Temporary* and *DJ Widow* this restriction does not hold, since the insignificance of the productivity estimate still does not exclude these categories from being case 4 households. However, if a transition occurs, that is, the interaction term becomes significantly positive, then an insignificant dummy variable unambiguously implies a case 4 household.

## 2.6 Specification of the empirical model

The economic analysis of production processes exhibits a close correspondence between theory and statistical analysis. Since the introduction of the Cobb-Douglas function in 1928, economists have developed a huge number of different functional forms with the aim to find a general function adhering to the properties derived from the theory of production. Although the Cobb-Douglas function has been widely used in the analysis of FHH farm efficiency (see Bindlish and Evenson 1993, Bindlish et al. 1993, Evenson and Mwabu 1998, Minot et al. 2000, Moock 1976, Saito et al. 1994), it is restricted in its generality due to its maintained hypothesis that the elasticity of substitution equals 1 (Fuss, McFadden and Mundlak 1978). Being concerned this feature might affect empirical results, Heady and Dillon (1961) introduced a second-degree polynomial in logarithms which was a taylor series approximation to an arbitrary production function. This function contains Cobb-Douglas as a special case, as it simply adds cross- and quadratic terms to the basic Cobb-Douglas function. In a series of papers which appeared a couple of years later, Christensen, Jorgenson, and Lau (1971a, 1971b, 1974) developed the same function and named it 'translog', which has partly replaced the Cobb-Douglas, due to its flexibility and its simple implementation as it is linear in parameters and can be conveniently estimated via standard estimation techniques.

A problem which is inherent to the empirical implementation of production functions in the context of cross-sectional household data is recursive causality. In most production settings, the input quantities must be considered as choice variables, because input quantities are chosen on past experience and thus on expected output. This implies that the choice of input quantities is not independent of the level of output. However, in this case, inputs are correlated with the error term. The same can be expected for all variable inputs where the decision on the quantities is likely to be determined by the expected amount or past realizations of output. Therefore, estimates from a production function using cross-sectional data should be treated with caution as the parameters are likely to be inconsistent due to the endogeneity of the independent variables (see Griliches and Mairesse (1998) for an extensive account of the problems involved when estimating production functions using cross sectional data).

The problem of endogeneity can be circumvented by estimating a cost function rather than a production function. When the optimization problem of the producer is reformulated such that the agent minimizes costs, given input prices, output quantities and a production technology, a cost function results. Under the assumption that farmers are price takers on a competitive market, output quantities are assumed to be exogenously given since in a competitive market the farmer chooses his output based on output prices which are exogenous as well (Jorgenson 1986). The fundamental result of duality theory is that the cost function is the dual formulation of the production function, that is, the same optimizing behavior leads to the same outcomes: minimizing costs at given prices implies maximizing production at given inputs (Fuss et al. 1978).[10] Under the assumption that the farm-households are price takers, all input prices can be treated as exogenous.

Productivity or efficiency can be decomposed into technical and allocative efficiency. However, the predictions based on the theoretical model developed in the previous section do not distinguish between the two kinds of efficiency. Higher productivity and output may be achieved by either better usage of existing inputs or by using more of one input. Therefore, to investigate the empirical content of the model, an approach is needed that can handle both technical and allocative efficiency. Other than the production function approach, the efficiency measurement embedded into a cost function is capable of capturing technical and allocative efficiency. A further advantage of the cost function is that it easily accommodates multi-output production schemes which is particularly relevant for societies dominated by agriculture as it is the case in Kenya.

In this study I focus on smallholder farming and exclude large commercial farms as these can be assumed to produce with a technology which is likely to differ substantially from those of the smallscale farmers. The median size of a

---

[10]Given parameter estimates of a cost function it is possible to construct the associated production function (Varian 1992).

smallscale farm in the sample is 3 hectares. All farms larger than the 95th percentile (22.5 hectares) are treated as large scale farms and are excluded from the sample.

Prices are available for hired labor and draft power. Prices for family labor are computed by the approach suggested by Jacoby (1993) and Skoufias (1994) while using the number of household members working in farming. Estimating family shadow wages is necessary in order to account for the observed difference between market wages and the family shadow price for labor (Menon, Perali and Rosati 2005). The data also contains information on hourly labor supply, but this data is considered extremely noisy as it is based on recall and is subject to a large number of missing cases. Furthermore, it covers only a week and does not account for any seasonal variations. Land is considered fixed, which is a reasonable assumption as land markets are largely unavailable in rural Kenya. I further consider fertilizer, pesticides and manure used, for which dummy variables are included when the respective input has been applied.

Since most households plant a relatively large portfolio of different crops, the output quantities are divided into three major output classes: maize and cereals, vegetables and fruits, and cash crops. As further controls for the choice of technology, I include a dummy for the educational background of the head of household (primary and secondary schooling) as well as dummy variables indicating whether the household applies labor intensive irrigation. Furthermore, a dummy has been included for households which have been visited by an extension agent. The translog variable cost function used here is given by

$$\ln VC = \alpha + \sum_{i=1}^{2} \beta_i \ln Q_i + \sum_{i=1}^{4} \gamma_i \ln P_i + \sum_{i=1}^{4} \delta_i \ln Y_i$$
$$+ \frac{1}{2} \sum_{i=1}^{2} \sum_{j=1}^{2} \phi_{ij} \ln Q_i \ln Q_j + \frac{1}{2} \sum_{i=1}^{4} \sum_{j=1}^{4} \eta_{ij} \ln P_i \ln P_j$$
$$+ \frac{1}{2} \sum_{i=1}^{4} \sum_{j=1}^{4} \rho_{ij} \ln Y_i \ln Y_j + \frac{1}{2} \sum_{i=1}^{2} \sum_{j=1}^{4} \psi_{ij} \ln Q_i \ln P_j \quad (10)$$
$$+ \frac{1}{2} \sum_{i=1}^{2} \sum_{j=1}^{4} \pi_{ij} \ln Q_i \ln Y_j + \frac{1}{2} \sum_{i=1}^{4} \sum_{j=1}^{4} \tau_{ij} \ln P_i \ln Y_j$$
$$+ \sum_{i=1}^{4} 0 \kappa_{ij} D_j$$

The variables are defined as follows:
$VC$: total variable cost (hired labor, draft, power, fertilizer, pesticides)

$Q_i$:  quantity of fixed inputs (land, household labor)

$P_i$:  price of variable inputs (daily wage rate, rental rate for draft power, fertilizer price, pesticides price)

$Y_i$:  output quantities (maize and cereals, vegetables and fruits, cash crops, milk)

$D_i$:  dummy variables capturing regional characteristics

Economic theory implies that the cost function must be homogeneous of degree one in prices such that if all prices increase by a factor $t$, then costs must increase by $t$ as well (see Varian 1992). This implies the following restrictions for the parameters of the translog cost function

$$\sum_{i=1}^{n} \gamma_i = 1, \quad \sum_{i=1}^{n} \eta_{ij} = \sum_{i=1}^{n} \rho_{ij} = \sum_{i=1}^{n} \tau_{ij} = 0 \quad (11)$$

## 2.7 Estimation the of stochastic frontier cost function

The cost function is estimated using a stochastic frontier approach, which has been established as a standard tool for investigating the production of cost efficiency (Kumbhakar and Lovell 2000). The stochastic frontier approach aims at estimating a cost or production frontier and to determine the distance of each farmer from the efficiency frontier. The empirical model is specified as

$$\ln VC = f(\boldsymbol{P}, \boldsymbol{Q}, \boldsymbol{Y}) + \nu + u \quad (12)$$

where $f(\cdot)$ is a function as specified by (10) and its arguments refer to prices, fixed inputs and output respectively. $\nu$ denotes a random component assumed to be distributed as $\nu \sim N(0, \sigma^2)$ and $u$ is a systematic measure of cost efficiency for which $u \geq 0$ must hold. Negative values for $u$ are prohibited since it is assumed that producers do not produce at negative costs. The interpretation of the efficiency measure $u$ is simple: since $f(\cdot)$ represents the efficiency frontier large values of $u$ imply large deviations from $f(\cdot)$ and therefore high levels of inefficiency. Since $u$ cannot become negative it needs to be modeled using an asymmetric distribution. The likelihood function constructed here is based on the exponential distribution, which is an asymmetric distribution and has achieved standard usage beside the half normal distribution.

A common approach is to estimate first the stochastic cost frontier to obtain estimates of $u$ which are in a second step regressed on a set of independent variables not included in the previous model. The efficiency measure is modeled as

$$u = \alpha + \sum_{k=1}^{K} X_k \delta_k + \eta \qquad (13)$$

where $X$ consists of (i) the FHH dummy indicators and (ii) the set of interaction terms, where income from other sources than farming is interacted with the FHH dummies to account for household specific levels of $p$. Off-farm activities include income from wage labor, profits from business and remittances. The properties of the measure of inefficiency imply that negative parameter estimates for $\delta_k$ are associated with greater efficiency.

The results of the cost frontier with restrictions (11) imposed are given in table 9 in the appendix. All signs are standard and no unusual parameter estimates call for explanation. As the results of interest are related to the second stage regression, I focus on these coefficients only. The results from the regression of the inefficiency term on the set of FHH dummies and the interaction terms are presented in columns 2 and 3 of table 5. The parameter of *DJ Widow* is negative and significant at the 10 percent level indicating that the average state of the household after controlling for alternative sources of income corresponds to case 4. The negative sign implies that given land endowments and prices *DJ Widow* households are on average more efficient compared to MHH. The coefficients of all other household categories do not achieve any usual level of significance. *DJ Widow* households are therefore not only more productive than MHH but also compared to the remaining FHH categories as well. Regarding case 4, the negative sign implies that the probability that these households are threatened by shortfalls of income and thus need to achieve higher levels of productivity is higher as compared to the other household categories. Since neither *DF Widows* nor *DJ Temporary* households are affected by low bargaining power, case 4 is ruled out and thus these households must be assigned to case 1. For the other for FHH categories it is not possible to determine the level of bargaining power beforehand, making it impossible to draw unambiguous conclusions. These household categories may either be equal to case 1 or case 4 households.

The interaction term for *DF Temporary* is significant and positive indicating that the low decision making competence increases farm inefficiency as soon as income from other sources rises. This result suggests a transition of *DF Temporary* households from case 4 to case 2. The insignificant parameter for the dummy variable may thus be interpreted such that in the first stage *DF Temporary* households correspond to case 4 where the effects induced by $p$ and $\theta$ neutralize each other, that is, the positive productivity effect emerging from low values of $p$ is compensated by the negative efficiency impact that arises from low values of $\theta$. *DJ Widow* households reveal a significantly positive parameter for the interaction term, too. Both cases are conform to the hypotheses that the negative impact of

Table 5: Estimates of production efficiency of different FHH categories

|  | Two-Stage | | Single-Stage | |
|---|---|---|---|---|
|  | Parameter | t-value | Parameter | t-value |
| *Dummy variables* | | | | |
| DJ Temporary | −0.009 | −0.375 | 0.016 | 0.259 |
| DF Temporary | −0.024 | −1.304 | −0.044 | −0.978 |
| DJ Widow | −0.031* | −1.731 | −0.094 ** | −2.090 |
| DF Widow | −0.001 | −0.052 | −0.033 | −0.820 |
| DJ Divorce | 0.058 | 0.859 | −0.034 | 0.708 |
| DF Divorce | 0.047 | 1.096 | 0.118 | 1.379 |
| Single | −0.033 | −0.486 | 0.147 | −0.200 |
| Polygamous | −0.023 | −0.866 | −0.043 | −0.711 |
| *Interaction terms* | | | | |
| DJ Temporary | 0.009 | 1.036 | 0.024 ** | 1.339 |
| DF Temporary | 0.017 ** | 3.769 | 0.034 ** | 2.930 |
| DJ Widow | 0.015 ** | 2.442 | 0.038 ** | 2.620 |
| DF Widow | −0.004 | −0.874 | −0.002 | 0.202 |
| DJ Divorce | −0.018 | −0.797 | −0.030 | −0.520 |
| DF Divorce | 0.002 | −0.180 | −0.005 | −0.183 |
| Single | 0.010 | 0.526 | 0.029 | 0.638 |
| Polygamous | 0.000 | −0.047 | −0.013 | −0.788 |

** parameter significant at 5 percent level
* parameter significant at 10 percent level

tenure insecurity on farming becomes increasingly apparent with rising $p$. However, tenure insecurity affects only households where women are left with low decision making power or where they are threatened of losing their land, that is, only households facing low levels of $\theta$ exhibit increasing inefficiency with rising off-farm incomes. All other households just achieve the same levels of average efficiency that characterizes MHH.

The approach of regressing the relative inefficiency term on a set of dependent variables not contained in the previous stochastic frontier estimate has been criticized. First, as the estimates of $u$ are obtained in a first stage and then regressed on further variables in a second step, the estimates of the second stage are inefficient. Secondly, an important condition under which this approach yields unbiased estimates is that the regressors contained in the first stage must be uncorrelated with the regressors of the second stage. If this condition is violated, the first stage estimators are biased. This condition is likely to be violated in the present setting as variables like land size are correlated with the different FHH categories (see table 3). However, biased estimates also yield biased estimates of the inefficiency terms. In order to assess the bias emerging from the correlation between first and second stage regressors, I substitute (13) for the inefficiency $u$ measure in (12), that is, I include the dummies along with the interaction terms in the first stage and treat these as technological parameters. This is a standard practice that has been pur-

Table 6: Estimates of production efficiency of single FHH indicator

| | Two-Stage | | Single Stage | |
|---|---|---|---|---|
| | Parameter | t-value | Parameter | t-value |
| *Dummy variables* | | | | |
| FHH | −0.136 | −1.415 | −0.030 | −1.222 |
| *Interaction terms* | | | | |
| FHH | 0.007 ** | 3.023 | 0.019 ** | 3.116 |

** parameter significant at 5 percent level
* parameter significant at 10 percent level

sued by other authors in other contexts as well (see Kumbhakar and Lovell 2000). The estimates are given in columns 4 and 5 of tables 5. The coefficients from the direct estimation of the cost function reveal some bias and inefficiency of the two-stage approach but basically confirm the results of the previous procedure. However, the parameter estimates of the significant coefficients more than double in absolute size and the dummy for *DJ Widows* becomes significant at the 5 percent level. The results therefore seem to be robust to different estimation approaches.

Given that the dependent variable is the logarithm of total variable costs, the parameters for can be interpreted as semielasticities. This measure gives the change of costs in percentage terms in response to a 1 unit change of the independent variable. However, for dummy variables one needs to do an adjustment to calculate the real the effect as suggested by Halvorsen and Palmquist (1980) and Kennedy (1981).[11] Applying the semielasticity to the estimates reveals that, at given outputs, being a *DJ Widow* household reduces cost by 8.8 percent. On the other hand, the parameters for the interaction terms can be treated as elasticities, since off-farm income enters the estimations in logarithmic form. A doubling of income, that is, an increase by 100 percent increases farming costs by 3.4 percent for *DF Temporary* households and by 3.8 percent for *DJ Widows*. This number needs to be interpreted in terms of the very low level of off-farm incomes, where a doubling of earnings is feasible, but still does not imply a substantial increase of welfare.

The contrasting signs of the dummy and interaction terms of *DF Temporary* and *DJ Widow* households imply a turning point in productivity at which house-

---

[11]The formula used for calculating the semielasticity for a dummy variable in a model with a logarithmic dependent variable is given by $g = 100(\exp(\hat{d} - frac12\hat{V}(\hat{d})) - 1)$, where $\hat{d}$ denotes the estimated dummy variable parameter and $\hat{V}(\hat{d})$ is its associated variance estimate.

Table 7: Labor supply and shares of income generating households

|  | Labor supply in hours per week and hectare | Share of households engaged in off-farm activities |
|---|---|---|
| MHH | 17.50 | 45.00 |
| FHH | 17.80 | 36.02 |
| DJ Temporary | 13.67 | 24.02 |
| DF Temporary | 19.37 | 36.91 |
| DJ Widow | 18.85 | 21.95 |
| DF Widow | 15.91 | 34.81 |
| DJ Divorce | N.O. | 28.00 |
| DF Divorce | N.O. | 49.35 |
| Single | N.O.† | 40.74 |
| Polygamous | 9.71 | 36.80 |

†N.O. indicates not sufficient observations.

holds 'switch' from greater to lower efficiency in the course of the transition from case 4 to case 2. The amount of log income per capita multiplied by the coefficient of the interaction term that equals the coefficient from the dummy variable in absolute size gives this turning point. For example, given the more reliable estimates of the latter approach, the estimate for this point is determined for *DJ Widows* by $0.094/0.038 = 2.47$ which equals 11.87 Kenyan shillings. The turning point is very low and *DJ Widow* households become immediately more inefficient compared to the average MHH as soon as any off-farm income becomes available. The same conclusion holds for *DF Temporary* households for whom the insignificant dummy implies a value of zero which suggests that the turning point is zero as well by resorting to the previous analysis. Column 3 in table 7 shows the share of households engaged in off-farm activities. For *DJ Widows* this share is particularly low compared to MHH but also with regard to the other FHH categories. Thus only a few of these households actually achieve the turning point. Although the share of *DF Temporary* is with 36.91 percent slightly higher, it is still low and thus only few households actually shift from one state into the other.

The results further suggest that FHH are not a homogeneous household category that can be simply aggregated to arrive at conclusions on productivity. Testing the equality of the parameters for the eight dummies does not reject the hypothesis that all coefficients are equal neither does a test for the equality of the interaction terms. However, testing whether the *DF Widow* and the *DJ Widow* interaction term have the same size yields a $\chi^1_2$-value of 4.86 which rejects the null of equal coefficients. An illustration of the problems arising from the heterogeneity of parameters is illustrated through the inclusion of a single FHH household dummy plus an additional interaction term in the second stage regression. The result is shown in line 1 and 2 of column 1 in table 6. The single FHH dummy that subsumes all different categories under a single indicator exhibits a negative sign, but does not become significant. The interaction term, on the other hand, is positive and significant at the 5 percent level. Also, the interaction term of the single FHH category covers up the six categories that revealed insignificant coefficients and thus hides the heterogeneity of the eight different classes. Furthermore, the single indicator does not offer an explanation other than *ad hoc* justification of the results, as it does neither account for different levels of bargaining power nor decision making authority.

The results call for an investigation of the source of the different productivity levels among FHH. The theory predicts that labor supply should systematically differ across households. Using the labor supply data provided in the WMS 3 weekly hours of labor supply per hectare of land are shown in table 7, while keeping in mind that these are likely to be subject to measurement error. The data show that the most productive household category *DJ Widow* also reveals almost the highest supply of household labor. Although this data must be interpreted with some caution, it is conform to the empirical results which established that *DJ Widow* are on average more productive than other household categories, if no offfarm income is available. Since, as discussed, also *DF Temporary* households are conform to case 4 when no other income but farming is available, the labor supply data also fits to these households, which exhibit the highest labor supply in the table. The labor supply data therefore further support the theory which predicts higher labor supply and greater levels of productivity among households located below their target income.

Table 8: Estimates of production efficiency of different FHH categories using dummy variables only

|  | Two-Stage | | Single-Stage | |
| --- | --- | --- | --- | --- |
|  | Parameter | t-value | Parameter | t-value |
| *Dummy variables* | | | | |
| DJ Temporary | 0.022 | 0.140 | 0.052 | 0.971 |
| DF Temporary | 0.014 | 0.900 | 0.028 | 0.730 |
| DJ Widow | −0.011 | −0.695 | −0.042 | −1.047 |
| DF Widow | −0.009 | −0.654 | −0.041 | −1.179 |
| DJ Divorce | 0.029 | 0.511 | 0.075 | 0.529 |
| DF Divorce | 0.042 | 1.270 | 0.133 | 1.638 |
| Single | −0.011 | −0.207 | 0.033 | 0.250 |
| Polygamous | −0.024 | −1.092 | −0.069 | −1.353 |

** parameter significant at 5 percent level
* parameter significant at 10 percent level

Finally, I investigate the impact of introducing the interaction terms in the model and re-estimate the same models presented above, but without the interaction terms. The results, presented in table 8 are striking. None of the dummy variables turns out to be significant indicating that the different effects emerging from $\theta$ and $p$ compensate each other. This finding emphasizes the necessity to control for the conditions under which FHH operate. Without the introduction of the interaction terms, the two household categories *DJ Widow* and *DF Temporary* would appear equally efficient as all other categories. One would conclude, that tenure insecurity does not pose to be a problem, which is not the case referring to the results from the previous analysis.

## 2.8 Conclusions

In this paper I have investigated the interrelatedness of response to tenure insecurity (and low decision power) and income risk. The results suggest that depending on which of these risks prevails, FHH are either less, equally or more productive compared to MHH. If the connection between these risks is not appropriately controlled for, empirical analysis would yield biased results. For the case of Kenya, FHH would seem equally productive compared to MHH and tenure insecurity would not appear to play a role in labor allocation decisions. Previous studies on this issue finding that FHH turn out to be even more productive (e.g. Moock 1976) do not offer an explanation for this finding and also seem to suggest that FHH fare better compared to MHH. However, the model developed in this paper shows that households are only more efficient when facing income risks and thus allows for explaining higher levels of productivity of FHH. Furthermore, the model allows to reconcile the finding of higher levels of productivity among FHH with the often repeated result that FHH are actually less productive, through integrating the concepts of income risk and tenure insecurity. Judging from the empirical results, both risks seem to be credible and FHH respond to them.

A second important result that came up in this study is that FHH categories are significantly different from each other, such that, when FHH are joined into a single household category, any analysis of productivity in rural areas falls short of capturing the specific constraints each of these household categories is facing. The results imply that tenure insecurity and the lacking ability to decide on investments are visible in only a few categories, revealing an impact on productivity in two household categories only. The findings are consistent with the assumption that male influence or bargaining power appears to be a factor that determines household production decisions. It is interesting to note that even within seemingly homogeneous categories like widows, divorced or temporary FHH there are significant differences. The findings suggest that a rethinking of the concept of FHH with regard to production and access to resources, but possibly also in the context of welfare, time use etc. would help to uncover structural discrimination and its sources.

The results point to the potential underestimation of the negative effects arising from tenure security when the FHH category specific constraints are not controlled for. This finding suggests that in previous studies the effect of tenure insecurity may turn out to be too low, which emphasizes the need and again raises the question for secure land right regimes for women and men. Only the granting of secure access to productive resources is a viable means to sustainably improve productivity of women in the long run. Insecure access to land has further implications as in rural areas it directly translates into the impossibility to obtain credits and to expand into further income generating activities. The finding that some FHH achieve higher production efficiency does not invalidate the necessity of targeted programs for women, but in view of the theory call for a refinement of the legal system and the status of women.

# A    Appendix 2.1

**Table 9: Estimates of the cost function parameters**

|  | Stochastic Frontier | | Constrained OLS | |
|---|---|---|---|---|
|  | Parameter | t-value | Parameter | t-value |
| lnland | −0.067 | −0.455 | −0.066 | −0.444 |
| lnhhlwage | 0.444 ** | 4.614 | 0.458 ** | 4.713 |
| lnwage | 0.528 ** | 5.551 | 0.515 ** | 5.365 |
| lntractor | 0.028 ** | 5.111 | 0.027 ** | 4.878 |
| pest | 0.049 | 1.307 | 0.050 | 1.332 |
| fert | −0.039 | −1.286 | −0.041 | −1.361 |
| prim | 0.002 | 0.088 | −0.007 | −0.307 |
| sec | 0.050 | 1.535 | 0.036 | 1.093 |
| extension | 0.044 | 1.329 | 0.046 | 1.406 |
| irrigate | 0.044 | 0.756 | 0.035 | 0.602 |
| manure | 0.094 ** | 2.931 | 0.098 ** | 3.068 |
| lnmaize | 0.248 ** | 2.792 | 0.248 ** | 2.793 |
| lnveggies | 0.174 ** | 2.639 | 0.168 ** | 2.551 |
| lncash | 0.218 | 0.691 | 0.222 | 0.707 |
| lab_land | −0.003 | −0.184 | −0.003 | −0.218 |
| lab_w | 0.016 | 1.457 | 0.013 | 1.199 |
| lab_t | −0.030 ** | −4.210 | −0.030 ** | −4.235 |
| lab_maize | −0.010 | −1.081 | −0.008 | −0.915 |
| lab_cash | −0.013 | −0.393 | −0.014 | −0.426 |
| lab_veg | −0.029 ** | −4.367 | −0.029 ** | −4.381 |
| land_w | 0.007 | 0.309 | 0.006 | 0.245 |
| land_maize | −0.004 | −0.678 | −0.004 | −0.661 |
| land_cash | −0.020 | −1.188 | −0.021 | −1.295 |
| land_veg | −0.002 | −0.358 | −0.001 | −0.243 |
| land_t | 0.009 | 0.545 | 0.009 | 0.562 |
| w_t | 0.040 ** | 4.328 | 0.041 ** | 4.328 |
| w_maize | −0.044 ** | −3.267 | −0.045 ** | −3.350 |
| w_cash | −0.019 | −0.294 | −0.021 | −0.330 |
| w_veg | −0.008 | −0.797 | −0.008 | −0.746 |
| t_maize | 0.001 | 0.137 | 0.002 | 0.206 |
| t_cash | −0.089 ** | −3.338 | −0.088 ** | −3.322 |
| t_veg | 0.018 ** | 2.408 | 0.019 ** | 2.500 |
| maize_cash | 0.043 ** | 5.530 | 0.044 ** | 5.607 |
| maize_veg | −0.048 ** | −19.135 | −0.049 ** | −19.154 |
| cash_veg | 0.005 | 0.717 | 0.005 | 0.671 |

—— Table continued on next page ——

—— Table continued from previous page ——

| | Parameter | t-value | Parameter | t-value |
|---|---|---|---|---|
| sqlnland | 0.006 | 1.023 | 0.006 | 0.983 |
| sqlnlabor | 0.014 | 1.360 | 0.017 | 1.618 |
| sqw | −0.056 ** | −3.425 | −0.055 ** | −3.318 |
| sqt | −0.010 * | −1.807 | −0.011 * | −1.955 |
| sqlnmaize | 0.062 ** | 27.784 | 0.062 ** | 27.515 |
| sqlncash | 0.059 ** | 3.723 | 0.059 ** | 3.755 |
| sqlnveggies | 0.036 ** | 18.786 | 0.036 ** | 18.687 |
| α | 3.406 ** | 11.454 | 3.442 ** | 11.564 |

** parameter significant at 5 percent level
* parameter significant at 10 percent level

# 3 Bargaining over Fertility in Rural Ethiopia

## 3.3 Introduction

Sub-Saharan Africa is characterized by exceptionally high population growth compared to other parts of the world. The Population Reference Bureau (2004) estimates, that between the late 1990s and the early 2000s population growth in sub-Saharan Africa amounted to 2.5% per annum, while for example population in Asia is growing at an annual rate of 1.6% (China excluded). High levels of population growth have induced policy makers to implement family planning programs all over the region, but with mixed results. As decisions over the desired number of children are intimately personal, it is difficult to directly address the demand for children. Hence, rather indirect measures need to be undertaken as spreading information on how to contracept and disseminate contraceptives. But the scope of policy options is limited if couples have differing preferences concerning their desired number of children. From the results of a number of studies it turned out that couples are unlikely to use contraceptives if only the woman and not the man wants to limit births (Dodoo 1992, Bankole and Singh 1998, Mesfin 2002, Short and Kiros 2002).

There is an ongoing debate on whether women and men have differing preferences over the number of children in general and if so how large the difference is. In an early review of the literature, Mason and Taj (1987) found that a general conclusion could not be drawn as the differences in preferences appeared to be small. The gap between women and men, however, seems to be greater in countries with high fertility rates, as compared to those where population growth is relatively low. In a more recent investigation, Bankole and Singh (1998) use DHS data to compare 13 African countries and find that in all of them men desire more children than women. The maximum difference is 3.9 children, reported from Niger.

In economic terms, the demand for children originates from the utility that parents derive from children. Different preferences therefore result from different costs and benefits that accrue to either women or men. In developing societies women have to carry the burden of pregnancy, delivery and most of the times care for the children. With every birth a woman puts her health (and life) at risk, as the supply of ante- and post-natal medical care is very low especially in rural areas. Women further incur the risk of short or long-term illnesses which are directly related to pregnancy. If the period between two births is not sufficiently long, the body cannot fully recover and the likelihood of falling sick increases. The same holds for low nutritional status (Mason and Taj 1987) which is frequent in rural areas and particularly so in rural areas of Ethiopia. Other costs accrue from the opportunity costs of caring for children. Since in the African context, couples often do not have a common budget (Doss 1996, Maluccio and Quisumbing 1999, Duflo and Udry 2004), women may not be compensated for income losses by their husbands. Having children on the other hand implies a number of benefits. Nugent (1985) has pointed out that children may be used as old-age security and cites some evidence that supports this hypothesis. Also, Caldwell (1986) reports that the resulting increase of the labor force due to an additional child rather benefits the husband. Children, if employed for household labor, rather help out on the farm instead of supporting women regarding household chores, while the additional income generated by that child does not necessarily benefit the wife. From a practical point of view, women have therefore a lower payoff from (i) having many children and (ii) from conceiving within a short period of time.

Knowledge of differing preferences is however not sufficient to make a statement on the true demand for children. When couples have differing preferences over the number of children and the time horizon in which they want to realize them, they must somehow come together and eventually arrive at a decision. The questions are, how large is the number of realized births and how is the decision achieved? How relevant are preferences of women? The answer to these questions is important because it can help to shape policies which aim at reducing the fertility rate. Any family planning policy not only needs to consider the prevailing desire for children, but also must acknowledge that this is a weighted average of individual preferences. In order to improve their efficiency, family planning programs must take into account how these weights are determined. If indeed, women have lower fertility preferences than men, then increasing the influence of women on household decision making would help to bring down the demand for children. Hogan, Berhanu and Hailemariam (1999) provide an example from Southern Ethiopia, where indicators of female autonomy are positively related to the use of contraceptives. Dyson and Moore (1983) and Murthi, Guio and Drèze (1995) found the same relationship to hold between autonomy and family planning in India.

The analysis of differing preferences among couples has attracted wide interest in the past. In contrast to the classic Beckerian household model, Manser and Brown (1980), McElroy and Horney (1981), Chiappori (1988, 1992), and Lundberg and Pollak (1993) have developed bargaining models that predict the outcomes of household decision making when preferences are not common. The underlying idea of these models is that household members do not necessarily share the same set of preferences but that household members may also have different weights in household decision making. The weights reflect the say of individuals in household decision making. The greater the weight—or in the parlance of the bargaining models, the bargaining power—the better an individual can accomplish personal interests. Empirical investigations frequently find support for the hypothesis that the household members' bargaining power influences the outcome of household decision making (see Fortin and Lacroix 1997, Browning, Bourguignon, Chiappori and Lechene 1994, Doss 1996, Browning and Chiappori 1998,

Thomas 1990, Maluccio and Quisumbing 1999, Haddad and Hoddinott 1994).

Based on these ideas, Eswaran (2002) introduced a model embedded in the Nash bargaining framework that describes the household decision making over fertility. In accordance to intrahousehold bargaining models, the number of children is a function of (i) the preferences of wife and husband, and (ii) the bargaining power of each of them. The preferences of wife and husband are determined by the costs and gains involved. Under the assumption that the costs of getting children are higher for women than for men, the model shows that increasing the intrahousehold bargaining power of women leads to lower levels of fertility.

Intrahousehold bargaining power of women can emerge out of many different ways. Female education is often considered as an important means of providing bargaining power (Mason and Taj 1987, Murthi et al. 1995, Sen 1997). Educated women often receive greater prestige and are in a better position to express their will and objections against putting their health at risk and further increases of their time burden. Women that have been exposed to education are more open to concepts associated to modernity and to modern means of contraception. Furthermore, the opportunity costs of time are higher for educated women since the options to find employment outside the household increase. Particularly wage labor is associated with higher returns from working and thus women's time becomes more valuable in monetary terms. Child care on the other hand increases the time burden and the need to reduce their employment activities.

The intrahousehold bargaining models discussed in the preceding paragraphs define bargaining power as the means to achieve utility if the individual were to leave the household and therefore rather focus on outside options. While education fits into that concept there are more options to define bargaining power in that way. Income earned by an individual is an example sometimes used in empirical studies (e.g., Thomas and Chen 1993) as a measure of bargaining power, which, in order to emphasize the importance of education, is closely related to that. Though conceptually appealing, in empirical work this measure turned out to be problematic (see discussion further below) and thus applied researchers have implemented other measures as well. The control over household assets is associated with an outside option if the individual retains control in case of dissolution of the household. Assets brought to marriage have been considered as a useful means to describe the outside options of an individual and, consequently, has been used in a number of empirical studies applying the concept of intrahousehold bargaining (Maluccio and Quisumbing 1999, Beegle et al. 2001).

In this study I look at household decision making and fertility goals in rural Ethiopia from two perspectives: (i) the impact of bargaining power on the decision to space births, which has turned out to be almost as important for the health of women and family planning as limiting births itself (Schultz 1993, Hogan et al. 1999) and (ii) the relationship between bargaining power and completed fertility. The first approach is based on a multistate model which is different from the usual static models that aim at predicting the number of children ever born conditional on a range of covariates. The second relies on count data regressions which is common in the analysis of fertility. The paper is structured in the following way: Section 2 briefly reviews the current situation regarding fertility in Ethiopia. Section 3 and 4 give an overview of the models and data used, and a description of the results. The paper concludes in section 5 with a summary.

## 3.3 Fertility in Ethiopia—the setting

Although the current population growth rate in Ethiopia is slightly below the sub-Sahara African average, the Ethiopian government considers the population growth rates still too high. With 72.4 million inhabitants the country has currently the second largest population in sub-Saharan Africa after Nigeria. The population growth rate is currently estimated to be 2.4 percent. According to UN population projections, the country would have in year 2050 the 10th largest population of the world (United Nations 2004). It should be noted here, that according to the World Development Indicators 2004 the population growth rate shows a declining trend from 1990 to 2002. The rates have been falling from 3.7% to 2.2% thus implying a demographic gift if this trend were to be continued (see Bloom and Williamson 1998). However, referring to data from the Population Reference Bureau (2004) this trend has been reversed in 2004. The total fertility rate that measures the number of children born to a woman during her lifetime is 5.9, which is above the sub-Saharan average of 5.6. The prevalence rate of contraceptive use is low: only 8% of all married women between 15 and 49 use any method of contraception. Sibanda, Woubalem, Hogan and Lindstrom (2003) report that the incidence of contraceptive use is substantially lower in Ethiopia as compared to other countries in sub-Saharan Africa. For example, the prevalence rate in neighboring Kenya is 39%. Burundi, which is even poorer than Ethiopia has a rate of 16%. In response to that, the Ethiopian government created in 1993 in the framework of the National Population Policy local population councils with the aim of increasing the use of contraceptives (National Population Policy of Ethiopia 1993, cited from Short and Kiros (2002)), but still with a low impact.

Maternal mortality in Ethiopia is high, and hence this is likely to influence the decision on how many children women want. The 2000 Demographic Health Survey (DHS) reports that 871 out of 100,000 births lead to the death of the mother.[12] Among the group of females aged 20 to 29, which is the age group in which most pregnancies occur, more than 30% of all deaths can be ascribed to maternal mortality. In rural areas, about 78% of pregnant women receive no antenatal care.

Fertility goals among couples differ. When asked in which time period women and men want to have their next child, substantially more men than women tend

---

[12]Treating every birth event as independent from each other and applying the probability of surviving a birth to the total fertility rate, the probability of surviving six births is 95%.

to have another child soon:[13] of couples that already have 5 children, 23.3% of men and 13.3% of women want another child soon. The DHS also reports large gender differences of the number of desired children. On average women desire 5.3 children while men want to have 6.4 children. Although these numbers vary across individual characteristics like age, education and the number of children already alive, the message remains the same: women prefer fewer children than men. In contrast to the findings from countries in Asia, Ethiopian couples do not exhibit preferences for sons (Short and Kiros 2002).

## 3.3 Methodological Problems of Analyzing Determinants of Fertility

The results from analyzing determinants of fertility are dependent on the measure of wanted fertility. The variation of the desired number of children across individual and household characteristics as reported in the DHS suggests that one should be cautious in interpreting these numbers: young couples' agreement tends to be higher as compared to older couples. The DHS data shows that among couples with only 2 children 76.6 percent of the women and 89.3 percent of men want more children while only 26.1 percent of women who conceived 6 children, want more as opposed to 48.2 percent of men who express their wish to get more children. Any analysis that relies on the number of desired children must take into account the possible fluctuation of preferences over time. Further, according to Bongaarts (1985) and Pritchett (1994) parents tend to rationalize the number of children ex-post, even if it actually exceeds their initially desired number of children. For most people, it is very difficult to state that a child is unwanted once it has been born. Statements on the desired number of children may therefore be flawed.

Another option is to use the observed number of children ever born to analyze fertility behavior. This approach is also subject to potential bias. Younger couples naturally have a lower number of children, as their family formation has just begun. Most studies using children ever born, try to account for this effect through including the age of wife and/or husband as an independent variable. This method disregards that young couples may rather want to postpone births instead of limiting the number of children. They may eventually have the same family size as older couples, but the younger couple achieves it at a later point of time. This has been reported to be the case in Africa, where contraceptives are often used for spacing births and not for limiting the number of children (Schultz 1993, Hogan et al. 1999, Westoff and Bankole 2001). When couples achieve their desired family size later, the inclusion of age gives the impression that younger couples prefer smaller families. Hence, studies relying on either the number of desired children

---

[13]The answer 'soon' refers to a period of less than 2 years.

or on the number of children ever born while not accounting for spacing effects use potentially biased data.

Economists investigating fertility rely on either static or dynamic models which impose different data requirements (Arroyo and Zhang 1997). Static models usually rely on information that is available in the current period of observation and are easy to handle, as count data models which are available in most statistical software packages can be applied. However, these models require information on completed fertility, that is, one needs to be sure that every woman considered in the sample does not get any more children in the future.

Dynamic approaches are often based on hazard rate models which estimate the elapsed time between two births.[14] An advantage of these models is that they allow for coping with censored data, that is, for couples who have not yet completed their family formation. To date, most authors applying hazard rate models ask for the time between marriage and first birth or the time between the $n$th and $n + 1$th birth (Andres and Urzua 2003, Arnstein and Altankhuyag 2001). This piecewise approach ignores the preceding birth events and is vulnerable to violations of a number of maintained assumptions (see Heckman and Walker 1990a). The model proposed by Heckman and Walker(1987, 1990a, 1990b) fully accounts for the whole birth history and can handle censored data (see also Newman and McCulloch (1984) for an alternative but less general model). A further advantage of this model is that it allows the variables in the conditioning set to vary over time, a feature which is not inherent in static models (see Klasen and Launov (2006) for an application of the Heckman-Walker model).

## 3.3 Birth Spacing

### 3.3.1 The Model

The model applied here belongs to the hazard rate family and enables to capture the dynamic nature of the birth process as well as the impact of bargaining power on transition from one birth parity to another and is based on Heckman and Walker(1987, 1990b, 1990a).[15] The basic idea is to model the entire birth history of a woman through a series of duration models while simultaneously accounting for (i) the probability that a woman stops her fertility cycle and (ii) the problem of censored observations. The latter aspect is particularly useful in the present study because the data consist of a single cross-section of observations from a household survey which was not primarily created to capture fertility.

---

[14] Hazard rate, survival or duration data models are build on the so called hazard function, which gives the probability that an individual remains in a certain state, e.g., the state to have 1 child, the state to have 2 children, and so forth. An increase of the hazard function implies that the time period between entering and leaving the state shortens and a decrease means the opposite.

[15] A parity denotes births attained.

The birth history is modeled as a finite-state continuous time process which starts at calendar time $\tau(0)$ when a woman enters her fertility cycle. After remaining childless for $t$ units of time, she conceives her first child denoted by $Y(1)$ at calendar time $\tau(1) = \tau(0) + t$. The set of birth states is discrete, that is $Y(\tau) \in \Gamma = 0, 1, 2, 3, \ldots, C$ and bounded from above ($C < \infty$). The elapsed time between two births is denoted by $T$, whereas $T_0, \ldots, T_C$ represents the entire duration from the time of entering the fertility cycle up to the last birth $C$. Note, that due to the right censoring of the data, the final state is $T_{\bar{C}}$, where $\bar{C}$ denotes the waiting time until the next birth, which may or may not occur. Let $H(\tau)$ be the set of $K$ covariates $x_k$ observed at calendar time $\tau$. The conditional hazard which denotes that a woman becomes at risk for the $j$th birth at time $\tau(j-1)$ is then given by

$$h_j(t_j|H(\tau(j-1)+t_j)), \quad j > 0 \qquad (14)$$

A useful feature of the conditioning set is, that for each period it potentially includes all past information up to $t_j$, that is all past changes of the social environment, the individual characteristics of the household and the woman herself can be captured.

Integration of (1) with respect to $t$ assuming that it is continuous yields the survivor function

$$S(h_j(t_j|H(\tau(j-1)+t_j))) = \exp\left(-\int_0^{t_j}(h_j(u|H(\tau(j-1)+u))du\right) \qquad (15)$$

which gives the probability that a woman remains childless up to $t$, or put differently the probability that she remains in the $j$th parity $j$ which can be written alternatively as

$$P(T_j > t_j|h_j(t_j|H(\tau(j-1)+t_j))). \qquad (16)$$

Multiplying the $j$th hazard by the $j$th survivor function gives the density of $t_j$ conditional on the covariates

$$g_j(t_j|H(\tau(j-1)+t_j)) = h_j(t_j|H(\tau(j-1)+t_j)) \cdot S_j(t_j|H(\tau(j-1)+t_j)) \qquad (17)$$

which forms the basis for the joint density observed at time $\tau(0) + \sum_{j=1}^{J} t_i$

$$g\left(t_1, \ldots, t_k|H\left(\tau(0)+\sum_{i=1}^{J}t_i\right)\right) = \prod_{j=1}^{C} h_j(t_j|H(\tau(j-1)+t_j)) \\ \times S_{j+1}(t_{j+1}|H(\tau(j)+t_{j+1})) \qquad (18)$$

where $C$ denotes the actual observed number of children. Note that after bearing $C$ children a woman made the transition from parity $j$ into parity $j+1$, which she may or may not end with another birth, which is captured by the survivor function $S_{j+1}(\cdot)$.

Modeling the birth history in the duration framework has the advantage that censoring of the data is explicitly accounted for through inclusion of the survivor function. As a woman enters the first parity at time $\tau(0)$ her actual number of children is observed at time $\tau(0) + \sum_{j=1}^{J} t_i$. The survivor function ensures that regardless of how many children a woman has born at the time of observation it is possible that she decides to have one birth more in the future. This feature of the model will be discussed in the section on estimation.

## 3.3 Unobserved Heterogeneity

The investigation of fertility behavior is usually made difficult due to presence of unobservables not captured by the conditioning set. Not accounting for these effects—here subsumed under $\theta$—may bias the estimated parameters. Considering unobserved effects is especially appropriate because apart from individual specific characteristics as infecundity, I do not have information on contraceptive practices.[16] Although the neglect of contraceptive use may not be too serious as the prevalence of contraceptives in Ethiopia is considerably below the Eastern African average (22%), the problem of unobserved infecundity remains. Furthermore, besides the use of modern methods of contraception, the amenorrheic period after birth may be artificially extended through breastfeeding which is also unobserved. These factors call for an explicit treatment of unobserved individual characteristics not contained in the data.

Heckman and Walker(1990b, 1990a) note, that unobserved heterogeneity $\theta$ may be divided into two components: (i) one that is observed by the woman but which does not appear in the data, and (ii) one that neither the analyst nor the woman observes. The first component may consist of effects like personal experience with usage of contraceptives or biological infertility. This information is unlikely to be available before the first parity, but in the second and every following transition a woman may build on this experience and change her behavior accordingly. This process may be depicted within the Bayesian framework where in every period $\theta$ is updated according to past experience. To avoid notational clutter, denote $x_j$ as the information set available at time $\tau(j-1) + t_j$. Define the probability measure of $\theta$ as $M(\theta)$ with density $m(\theta)$ and $supp\ M(\theta) = \Theta$, then the density of $\theta$ for parity $i$ conditional on the previous duration $t_{j-1}$ is given by

$$m_j(\theta|t_{j-1}, x_{j-1}) = \frac{m_{j-1}(\theta)g_1(t_{j-1}|x_{j-1}, \theta))}{g_{j-1}(t_{j-1}|x_{j-1}, \theta)}. \qquad (19)$$

---

[16]The 1995 round of the survey provides information on current uses of contraceptives. This however does not necessarily represent past behavior, since the introduction of modern contraceptives is often a recent phenomenon and forced by governmental Family Planning programs which take place with different regional intensity.

The insight provided by the assumption of Bayesian learning is that women's decisions about current parities is affected by the experiences she made during past birth intervals. To account for the Bayesian updating process the mean of previous durations is included in order to capture experience effects that would otherwise be attributed to unobserved heterogeneity. The second part of the heterogeneity which is left for specification is assumed to be time invariant and is modeled as a mixture distribution given by

$$g\left(t_1, \ldots, t_k | H\left(\tau(0) + \sum_{i=1}^{J} t_i\right)\right) = \int_\Theta \prod_{j=1}^{C} g(t_j | H(\tau - 1) + t_j) dM(\theta) \quad (20)$$

$\theta$ in this respect is time invariant and captures any peculiarities which are not covered by the independent variables in the conditioning set and are not known to the women as well to the researcher.

## 3.3 Estimation

In their work on fertility in Sweden, Heckman and Walker (1990b) as well as Klasen and Launov (2006) for the case of the Czech Republic extended the survivor function to include the possibility of stopping the birth process. The stopping behavior is modeled as a mixture between the probability that a woman decides to have no more children and the probability that she continuous the transition process up to an unknown time. Denote the probability that a woman stops child bearing for any reason (biological or behavioral) after the $j$th birth with $P_j$. Then the conditional survivor function of parity $j$ can be written as

$$S_j(t_j | H(t), \theta) = P_j + (1 - P_j) \exp\left\{-\int_0^{t_j} h_j(u | H(t), \theta) du\right\} \quad (21)$$

The densities of $t$ are modeled using a Weibull distribution which has only positive support as required and has the conditional density

$$g(t|x_i, \beta) = \exp(x_i'\beta)\alpha t^{\alpha-1} \exp[-\exp(x_i'\beta)t^\alpha] \quad (22)$$

The Weibull distribution contains an additional parameter $\alpha$, which measures the duration dependence of the current parity. The hazard $h(t)$ yields positive duration dependence if $dh(t)/dt > 0$ which holds for $\alpha > 1$. A positive duration dependence implies, that with the time periods becoming longer, the probability of exiting the state increases. It is principally possible to condition $P_j$ on a number of independent variables using a logistic density function as has been done by Heckman and Walker (1987). Unfortunately, this approach bears some problems in the present setting, as it is very rare in rural areas, that couples stop the birth process deliberately after only one, two or even three children. The application further requires the introduction or more variables in the conditioning set of the quit function $P_j$. In order to avoid an overparameterization of the model and to save degrees of freedom I do not put emphasis on implementing the conditioning of $P_j$ on further variables. However, I present the results of a hazard model where the quit probabilities from the third birth onwards are modeled using a logistic function of the form

$$P_j = \frac{1}{1 + \exp(-x'_j \phi)} \qquad (23)$$

in order to investigate the robustness of the results.

In the presence of time invariant unobserved heterogeneity, one needs to consider the distribution of $\theta$. In a similar approach as the one presented here, Newman and McCulloch (1984) assume the heterogeneity to pursue a certain parametric distribution and obtain the likelihood by integrating out $\theta$. This approach, though common in many applications, has been demonstrated by Heckman and Singer (1984) to be vulnerable to misspecification of $M(\theta)$. To avoid bias in the estimation of the parameters, the likelihood here is maximized as a finite mixture, where no parametric form of $M(\theta)$ needs to be specified. In finite mixture models, one assumes that $m(\theta)$ has a finite set of support points $\theta$, to which the probabilities $\pi$ are attached (see McLachlan and Peel (2000) and Lesperance and Lindsay (2001) for expositions of the method). In other words one assumes that the population from which the random variable $t_j$ is drawn can be decomposed into $m$ distinct subpopulations. The probability that $t$ is drawn from the $m$th subpopulation (or component) is given by $\pi_i$, whereas $\sum_{i=1}^{M} \pi_i = 1$ and $\pi_i \geq 0$. The $\theta$'s can be understood as parameters which capture the subpopulation characteristics. As the number of subpopulations is unknown, it has to be estimated, which is done by adding support points to the model and choosing the optimal number of points on the basis of an information criterion like the Akaike or the Schwartz criterion.[17] Using the new survivor function given by (21) the contribution of the $i$th woman to the likelihood is

$$\mathcal{L}_i = \sum_{m=1}^{M} \left\{ \prod_{i=1}^{\bar{C}} \left[ -\frac{\partial \ln S_j(t_j|H(\tau));\theta_i)}{\partial t_j} \right] S_j(h_j(t_j|H(\tau));\theta_i) \right\}^{b_1}$$
$$\times S_{j+1}(t_{j+1}|H(\tau);\theta_i)^{b_2} \pi_m \qquad (24)$$
$$= \sum_{m=1}^{M} \prod_{i=1}^{\bar{C}} g(t_j|H(\tau))^{b_1} \cdot S_{j+1}(t_{j+1}|H(\tau);\theta_i))^{b_2} \pi_m$$

where the $b$'s denote indicator functions $b_1 = 1[\bar{C}]$ and $b_2 = 1[C]$. The log-likelihood is maximized applying an EM-algorithm proposed by Dempster, Laird

---

[17] See Leroux (1992) for a formal justification of the use of information criteria to evaluate the number of components in a mixture model.

and Rubin (1977). To implement the EM-algorithm consider the following general format

$$\mathcal{L} = \sum_{m=1}^{M} \prod_{m=1}^{N} \pi_m^{d_{jm}} [f_m(t; \beta_m)]^{d_{jm}} \qquad (25)$$

where $d_{jm}$ denotes an indicator variable that takes on the value 1 if $t_j$ is drawn from the $m$th subpopulation and zero else. Although $d_{jm}$ is not observed one can calculate its expected value through

$$E(d_{jm}) = P(d_{jm} = 1|t_j) = \hat{d}_{jm} = \frac{\pi_m f_m(t_j; \beta_m)}{\sum_{m=1}^{M} \pi_m f_m(t_j; \beta_m)} \qquad (26)$$

Using (26) the posterior probability that $t_j$ belongs to the $m$th subpopulation is given by

$$\hat{\pi}_m = \sum_{j=1}^{N} \hat{d}_{jm}/n \qquad (27)$$

Estimation of the parameters of the likelihood function proceeds with a given initial starting value of $\beta_m$ and $\pi_m$ from which the log-likelihood is formed as

$$\ln \mathcal{L} = \sum_{j=1}^{M} \sum_{i=1}^{N} \hat{d}_{im} [\ln f_m(t_i; \beta_m) + \ln \pi_m] \qquad (28)$$

Because $d_{im}$ is also unknown it is replaced by its expected value $\hat{d}_{jm}$ which leads to the E-step in the EM-algorithm. In the M-step one maximizes (28), obtain new estimates of $\pi$ and $\beta$, calculate $\hat{d}_{jm}$ using these estimates and (26), insert them back into (28) and maximize again. These iterations are repeated until a previously defined stopping criterion is met.[18] Unfortunately, the EM-Algorithm is vulnerable to the choice of starting values and it is not sure whether one finds the optimum by repeated random starts. To account for this shortcoming, I apply a simulated annealing global maximization algorithm (Goffe, Ferrier and Rogers 1994) in order to find a good set of starting values.[19] For inference on the parameters, McLachlan and Peel (2000) suggest to bootstrap the standard errors. As the model number of parameters is large, the computation time needed is too long to bootstrap the standard errors as a single solving amounts to 36 hours. As an alternative I apply the robust Huber-White sandwich estimator (Huber 1967, White 1982). This completes the estimation process the results of which are presented below. All programming necessary has been done using Ox version 3.40 (see Doornik 2002).

---

[18] The stopping criterion used here is based on the predicted final likelihood as described in Lesperance and Lindsay (2001).
[19] I have implemented the MaxSa code provided by Charles Bos.

## 3.3 Results

The results of the hazard model are presented in table 3.2. Using the information criteria, a two component model was selected. The components are not easy to interpret as they may capture different effects. The probabilities attached to the support points roughly divide the sample into two halves, which is too large to be explained by contraceptive users and non-users alone. The components may capture regional differences as well as temporary infecundity. The results do further not allow for a clear-cut answer on the impact of female bargaining power on household decision making. The respective parameters (*BP Wife*) are positive in all but the sixth parity, which would suggest that women's bargaining power increases the probability of an early birth and thus shortens the time between two consecutive births. However, only the female bargaining power parameter of the fifth parity is significant. The coefficients denoting male bargaining power are positive and significant at the 5 percent level in 5 cases.

At first sight these results contradict the assumption of the presence of intrahousehold bargaining over fertility. It may be noted, however, that in all but the first case the parameter denoting bargaining weights of men is larger as compared to that of women, implying that the impact of assets brought to marriage is larger for men.[20] A Wald test of equality of the female and male bargaining power indicators yields a value of $\chi_6^2 = 24.064$ and which leads to rejection of the null of equal parameters. Also, the female bargaining power parameters exhibit a declining trend with later births. The impact of male bargaining power first increases in magnitude up to the third birth until it remains stable at the following parities. However, in total, these results are not sufficient to unambiguously support the hypothesis of an intrahousehold bargaining over spacing of births.

The age difference reveals an unexpected sign and is significant for five parities. Larger differences between husband and wife largely imply longer time spells between births. This result may be explained by declining fertility of men at older ages. However, the age difference is positive and significant for the first parity indicating that equally aged couples wait longer. This might have to do with the widespread traditional marrying habits, where young girls are married to older men by her parents. The education effects of women are also unexpected, that is, with higher education women experience births at a faster rate. However, for the first birth, female education lengthens the waiting time for the first child. Previous marriages and children lengthen the periods for first birth in the current partnership. This effect is however leveled at later parities. Such ambiguous effects are not uncommon for studies on fertility in Africa (Benefo and Schultz 1996, Anker and Knowles 1982), where male education sometimes leads to higher fertility and shorter intervals between two births. However, the results obtained may be spuri-

---

[20]Note, that this assertion is based on the assumption that a parameter not significantly different from zero equals zero.

ous, due to the very low educational background of the women in the sample. The income effects are ambiguous and do not yield a consistent picture as they exhibit a switch across parities. The results, however, establish the tendency, that at later parities the income parameters predict that the probability that a woman leaves a state decreases at higher levels of income. That is, wealthier couples prefer longer periods between adjacent births. The results of the impact of education are mixed. Female and male education reveal in most cases a negative sign, although some parities exhibit a significantly positive parameter.

The impact on duration emerging from the death of a child is as expected. The parameter *Died* is significantly different from zero in all but the last parity and yields a negative sign, indicating that the death of a child lengthens the time interval between adjacent (alive) births. Expected village child mortality reveals the expected positive sign for early parities at which it achieves a 5 percent significance level: higher expected mortality rates lead couples to have children earlier and in shorter time periods. However, after having achieved a certain number of children, this effect loses importance and does not become significant. Older cohorts do significantly exhibit negative signs, implying that couples who have started the birth process before or at early phases of the Ethiopian political and economic crisis have longer waiting times. Southern regions are indicative for shorter birth intervals, which is in line with the expectations. Tigreans reveal longer waiting times for the first parity, although the sign switches for consecutive periods where the coefficient becomes significant at two parities.

Finally, the $\alpha$'s need to be interpreted. All are highly significant and greater 1, which means that all parities are subject to positive duration dependence. As noted above, positive duration dependence implies that with increasing passing of time since the last birth, the probability increases of leaving the current parity. This effect is plausible given the large family sizes. The positive duration dependence is also reflected by the low values of the quit probabilities for the first parities. The quit probabilities are increasing with later waiting times as is to be expected. That is, with increasing number of children, the likelihood that couples stop the fertility process increases. In sum, the several hints combined do not reveal a unique picture of the household decision making process, though the bargaining power parameters show a tendency, as the results on wife's and husband's bargaining power reflect some disparity on the household decision over fertility. Furthermore, the more liberal North shows some tendency to support longer waiting times. However, to arrive at a conclusion on the presence of intrahousehold bargaining, the statistical results do not suffice as a basis to unambiguously support the hypothesis that wives bargain with their husbands over the spacing of births.

To investigate the robustness of the previous results, I further present in table 3.3. the estimates of a hazard model where the quit probabilities from the third birth onwards are conditioned on a set of independent variables. The set of variables is the same as the one chosen for the hazard model. The estimates of the extended hazard model are very close to the previous coefficients and no substantial changes are obvious. The results regarding the quit probabilities do not yield consistent results as the signs, sizes and significance levels substantially change between parities. This finding can be most likely explained with an overparameterization of the model, that leads to a substantial loss of degrees of freedom.

The failure of the dynamic model to generate unambiguous results also needs to be interpreted in view of Ethiopian history. In the past decades Ethiopia has experienced a number of events which render the analysis of fertility in a dynamic context difficult. First, the reign of Haile Selassie was overthrown in 1974 in a coup d'etat by the military which in the following 15 years substantially changed the health system and introduced first steps toward family planning. In the 80's, Ethiopia was hit by several severe famines in which an estimated 400,000 people died of starvation and related diseases. When the military or Derg regime took power, it engaged in a war with the Eritrean independence movement which lasted until 1989 and preliminarily ended with proclamation of Eritrea as an independent state. All those events can be assumed to have exerted an influence on fertility patterns of Ethiopian couples. Though the fighting during the war as well as the famines have been regionally concentrated, its impact on the population is likely to be similar across regions (Lindstrom and Berhanu 1999). Nationwide, fertility rates substantially fluctuate during the times of political and economic crisis. Fertility is often treated as a response to risks where children serve as an informal insurance and thus insecurity should increase fertility rates. On the other hand, malnutrition and psychological stress emerging from hunger and war lead to an increase of infecundity. It is obvious from the results that women who entered the fertility cycle before the regime switch exhibit a different fertility pattern as women who formed a couple afterwards.

## 3.3 Number of Children

### 3.3.1 The Model and Estimation

In this section, I turn to the estimation of the effects of bargaining power on the number of children. To arrive at data on completed fertility, I construct a new data set where women under age 45 are excluded. Beyond this age, the likelihood that the woman gives birth to a child is only 2% (Hotz, Klerman, Alex and Willis 1993). A more conservative measure would be to exclude women younger than 49, but in order to save observations the lower threshold appears to be appropriate. The results hold, however, when the threshold is shifted to age 49.

The new sample comprises 203 observations. None of the women included has any reported educational background, which is why only husbands' education is considered.[21]

Because the dependent variable consists now of the number of children ever born, the distribution is assumed to be Poisson, which has density

$$f(y_i) = \frac{\mu_i^{y_i} e^{-\mu_i}}{y_i!} \qquad (29)$$

where $\mu_i$ is modeled as $\mu_i$ by $\mu_i = \exp(x_i'\beta)$. Despite its restriction that the mean and variance are implicitly assumed to be equal (in this case the data is said to be equidispersed), the Poisson distribution has a number of advantages. First, the Poisson maximum likelihood estimator (MLE) is most efficient if the dependent variable $y$ is Poisson distributed, and second even if the assumption that $y$ follows a Poisson distribution is violated, the Poisson MLE is still consistent (Wooldridge 2002, p. 649). As noted, a shortcoming of the Poisson distribution is its implicit assumption of equidispersion, which is inherent to the functional form. A violation of equidispersion does however harm the estimation of the standard errors of the parameters.

The dependent variable displays overdispersion with variance-mean ratio of $8.431/4.344 = 1.940$. In this case the appropriate model choice would be the Negative Binomial (NB) model, which offers a more flexible way to model the variance and thus can handle overdispersion.[22] However, the efficiency of the estimates is lower as well as its robustness to violations of the functional form, which why the presence of overdispersion should always be tested as it may disappear once the dependent variable is conditioned on a set of regressors. To investigate the overdispersion of the dependent variable, I conduct a simple regression based test suggested by Cameron and Trivedi (1998) that checks the validity of the Poisson distribution against the alternative Negative Binomial distribution. The test rejects the hypothesis of overdispersion in favor of equidispersion;[23] the $\alpha$-value obtained is $-0.0004$ (with a standard error of $0.037$) which is decisively insignif-

---

[21] I have also included a set of village dummies which led to a slight decrease of the standard errors of the remaining parameters, but did not turn out to become significant themselves. Based on the results of an Akaike information criterion which indicated the superfluency of the dummies, I decided to drop these variables as they did not substantially affect the parameter size of the other variables.

[22] Further flexible approaches have been proposed by Winkelmann and Zimmermann (1995), Famoye (1992), Famoye (1993), and Wang and Famoye (1997). These models have the advantage of being capable to deal with either under- or overdispersion.

[23] The test procedure is appropriate to detect either over- or underdispersion. Let $\hat{\mu}_i$ be the predicted value of the dependent variable $y$ using the Poisson model. Then the test can be conducted by regressing

$$\frac{(y_i - \hat{\mu}_i)^2 - y_i}{\hat{\mu}_i} = \alpha \hat{\mu}_i + u_i \qquad (30)$$

If $\alpha > 0$ the data is overdispersed and if $\alpha < 0$ the data is underdispersed, which can be tested by using a simple t-test.

icant. The test results speak in favor of the Poisson model which is more efficient than the alternative NB model. In a first step I therefore apply a simple Poisson model with standard errors based on the Huber-White sandwich estimator. I also estimate an NB model to investigate whether overdispersion has really no effect.

### 3.3.2 Results

Table 13 reports the estimated parameters of the Poisson model. First of all, the impact of bargaining power of both, women and men, on the number of children is striking. The parameter of *BP Wife* is negative while *BP Husband* is positive and both are significantly different from zero at the 5 percent level. The estimates indicate that with increasing bargaining power of women, families have fewer children. In contrast to that, family size increases with rising male bargaining power. Testing the null of equal parameters using a Wald test yields a $\chi_1^2$-value of 8.67 thus rejecting the null at the 1 percent level. The contrasting signs are conform to the hypothesis of an intrahousehold bargaining process on the number of children. The coefficient capturing age differences is negative, but insignificant.

Previous marriages per se do not affect the number of children—neither for women nor for men. The impact of education of the husband is positive, but not significant. None of the parameters representing income is significant, too. The women's age also significantly affects family size: relatively younger mothers do have less children. The final two indicators that are included to capture women's status *Tigray* and *South* reveal both a positive sign although the former is insignificant. However, the parameter southern groups is significant and reveals that women appear to have a low say on household decision making. The effect of village mortality is significant, too, indicating the village mortality induces a 'hoarding' effect.

Although the statistical testing rendered the Poisson model the better choice, I estimate a Negative Binomial model in order to compare whether the results are robust to the possible overdispersion. The NB model I use incorporates a variance function of the form

$$\sigma^2 = \mu + \alpha \mu^2 \qquad (31)$$

If $\alpha = 0$ the NB distribution reduces to the Poisson form. A further test can therefore be based on checking whether $\alpha$ is equal to zero. The results are presented in table 14 and establish that overdispersion does not determine the results. The parameter $\alpha$ is very small and does not reveal a substantial deviation from the Poisson model although the estimate is significant at the 5 percent level. However, the estimates are very similar to the Poisson estimates and allow for the same conclusions presented above.

The results discussed so far may be subject to unobserved heterogeneity for similar reasons as in the hazard model. Women may have become infecund before achieving the desired number of children or use contraceptives in order reduce unwanted fertility. To account for these unobserved factors the model is again estimated as a finite mixture model, but of a slightly different form. The model is not cast into the form of a random intercept model as has been done with the hazard model before, but to account for the heterogeneity a full set of parameters is estimated for each sub-population. It is assumed that the data is drawn from two ($M$) entirely distinct populations with density

$$f(\theta; x) = \sum_{i=1}^{M} \lambda_i f_i(\theta_i; x), \quad 0 < \lambda_i < 1, \quad \sum_{i=1}^{N} \lambda_i = 1 \qquad (32)$$

where $f_i(\cdot)$ denotes the Poisson density for the $i$th sub-population from which the sample is drawn with probability $\lambda_i$. Using (32), the household specific density becomes

$$\ell_i = \sum_{i=1}^{M} \lambda_i \frac{\exp(x_i'\theta)^{y_i} \exp(-\exp(x_i'\theta))}{y_i!} \qquad (33)$$

(33) is estimated using the EM-algorithm again, so that the general form of the function that is maximized is the same as given by (28). The results from a two component model are reported in table 15. A comparison of the Akaike information criteria yielded by the two models renders the two component model the better choice indicating that unobserved heterogeneity like differential exposure to contraceptives, infecundity, or access to health facilities might have an impact on the results. The previous findings of the differential impact of bargaining power on family size find again support in both components. All bargaining power coefficients are significant at least at the 10 percent level. The female coefficient in the first component group even becomes substantially larger in absolute value than in the previous single component model. The same observation holds for the male bargaining power parameter. In the first component, previous marriages and children from previous relations become significant. The signs for the children are rather unexpected as couples with previous children have significantly more children in current relations. This finding is difficult to interpret. One possible explanation is that couples in this group do not consider children from previous marriages as part of their fertility goal. This would imply, starting the whole birth process from zero when a new marriage begins. Such behavior would seem rational in the current setting, if children stay with the former partner. However, the probability that a household belongs to the first component is rather small and amounts to 30 percent. Furthermore, the results regarding the bargaining power parameters do not change.

The results presented in this section differ from the results obtained on the timing of births, which do not show an unambiguous impact of bargaining power on birth spacing. Part of the problem might arise from the time horizon that both models cover. While the count data model is restricted to women older than 45, the hazard model considers also the recent past, that is, women who just entered their fertility cycle. An explanation for the differing results might be that preferences for birth spacing have changed over time. Younger women may prefer to achieve their fertility goals faster as compared to older mothers. An explanation for this might be found in changes of the provision of health care. In 1983 the government approved a ten year health sector development plan and since then, the Ethiopian health care system has experienced some improvements in the sector of pre- and post-natal care (Kello and Papagallo 1997). Unfortunately, it is not possible to control for this effect unless data is available on the establishment of hospitals and other health services.

## 3.3 Conclusions

This study looks at the impact of intrahousehold bargaining power on household decision making over fertility. Two aspects have been considered: the time intervals between births and the total number of children after completing the fertility cycle. In view of differing preferences on the number of children, it was expected that the individual bargaining position determines the leeway to accomplish personal fertility goals. The results of the birth history model do not reveal a clear relation between female autonomy and the spacing of births. The impact of male bargaining power on the timing of births, however, is larger as compared to women's bargaining power. The statistical difference of the parameters implies that there is still not necessarily full agreement on the timing of births. On the other hand, the results show that regarding the number of children, high bargaining power of women decreases family size while male bargaining power increases it. The result is robust to different estimation approaches that account for unobserved heterogeneity. The inconsistency of the results might be explained by changing preferences over time, that is, younger couples may prefer to achieve their fertility goals earlier and this change might have driven the results. Such changing differences may come about, for example, from improvements in pre- and post-natal health care.

The findings presented here suggest that in order to effectively reduce fertility, public family planning programs need to address women and men simultaneously: men because their opposition to family planning is an important reason for not using contraceptives to space or limit births (Hogan et al. 1999). Women, since their low bargaining power hinders them to accomplish their reproductive goals. The fact that female autonomy is related to lower fertility also opens the door for other means to reduce fertility rates, e.g., through improving the bargaining position of women thus enabling them to push their goals through. This may be achieved via the development of labor markets that enable women to generate off-farm personal income. In other settings, personal income has been demonstrated to be correlated with impact on household decision-making (see Browning et al. 1994, Browning and Chiappori 1998, Thomas and Chen 1993). Although education did not turn out to be a determinant of prolongation and the number of births, it may nevertheless be important in the presence of income earning opportunities outside the household. As the case of Kerala in India demonstrates, fertility rates decline when women find better outside options in terms of earning income and participation in political decision making (Murthi et al. 1995, Sen 1997). From this perspective, an improvement of education for women and girls must go hand in hand with the development of labor markets. Without the prospect to generate income it is likely that the impact of education is lower as if there were job opportunities outside the household.

The results further emphasize the many facets of bargaining power and the bargaining process itself, which renders the operationalization of the bargaining power difficult. Personality, economic environments, or cultural traditions that define the role of the women in family and society are likely to influence the women's bargaining position, making it difficult to construct a unique indicator that allows for capturing all determinants. Addressing the multidimensionality of bargaining power therefore requires to include variables that account for the cultural background of the woman as has been done in this study. Nevertheless, more knowledge on the determinants of bargaining power would be desirable in order to (i) construct better measures and (ii) to explore further options that induce social change.

# A Appendix 3.1.

Table 10: Means and descriptions of variables

| | Birthinterval† | BP Wife | BP Husband | Durat | Died |
|---|---|---|---|---|---|
| | | Dynamic data | | | |
| Parity 1 | 78.00 | 0.11 | 0.86 | -* | 0.19 |
| Parity 2 | 36.00 | 0.17 | 1.30 | 6.90 | 0.08 |
| Parity 3 | 36.48 | 0.21 | 1.52 | 5.93 | 0.04 |
| Parity 4 | 36.00 | 0.25 | 1.73 | 6.65 | 0.03 |
| Parity 5 | 33.60 | 0.27 | 1.93 | 4.69 | 0.03 |
| Parity 6 | 33.96 | 0.29 | 2.11 | 4.44 | 0.01 |

| | | Time invariant data | |
|---|---|---|---|
| Age difference | 8.30 | Age difference | |
| Educ. wife | 1.68 | Education in school years | |
| Educ. husb. | 2.45 | Education in school years | |
| Married wife | 0.24 | Wife had previous relation | |
| Married husb. | 0.44 | Husband had previous relation | |
| Child wife | 0.27 | Wife's children from previous relation | |
| Child husb. | 0.46 | Husband's children from previous relation | |
| Older 40 | 0.38 | Age chohort older than 40 years | |
| Inc. Quart. 1 | 0.18 | Lowest income quartile | |
| Inc. Quart. 2 | 0.27 | Medium income quartile | |
| Inc. Quart. 3 | 0.27 | Medium income quartile | |
| Village Mort. | 0.07 | Expected child mortality rate | |
| Tigray | 0.11 | | |
| South | 0.39 | | |

† Medians reported
* No data available

Table 11: Jointly estimated parameters of all parities

|  | Param. | t-value | Param. | t-value | Param. | t-value |
|---|---|---|---|---|---|---|
|  | First Birth | | Second Birth | | Third Birth | |
| Alpha | 2.224 ** | 38.263 | 2.239 ** | 38.837 | 2.234 | 34.326 |
| Constant | -5.890 ** | -30.338 | -5.492 ** | -26.941 | -4.848 ** | -23.225 |
| BP Wife | 0.056 | 1.452 | 0.039 | 1.290 | 0.000 | 0.003 |
| BP Husband | -0.011 | -0.389 | 0.101 ** | 4.103 | 0.172 ** | 8.210 |
| Prev. Duration | | | 0.113 ** | 13.112 | 0.004 | 0.213 |
| Died | -0.582 ** | -5.998 | -1.194 ** | -8.206 | -1.308 ** | -6.619 |
| Agedifference | 0.020 ** | 4.202 | -0.022 ** | -3.568 | -0.054 ** | -7.424 |
| Educ. wife | -0.268 ** | -2.257 | 0.524 ** | 4.042 | 0.442 ** | 2.834 |
| Educ. husb. | 0.253 ** | 2.885 | -0.137 | -1.469 | -0.687 ** | -6.175 |
| Married wife | -0.183 ** | -3.998 | 0.112 ** | 2.313 | 0.093* | 1.692 |
| Married husb. | -0.181 ** | -3.954 | 0.114 ** | 2.354 | 0.095* | 1.728 |
| Child. wife | -0.156 ** | -3.529 | -0.173 ** | -3.270 | 0.316 ** | 4.547 |
| Child. husb. | -0.038 | -0.938 | -0.013 | -0.293 | -0.101 ** | -2.094 |
| Older 40 | -1.268 ** | -15.005 | -1.080 ** | -10.422 | -0.706 ** | -6.243 |
| Inc. Quart. 1 | -0.108 | -0.956 | 0.046 | 0.372 | -0.042 | -0.304 |
| Inc. Quart. 2 | -0.253 ** | -2.578 | -0.188* | -1.783 | -0.245* | -1.910 |
| Inc. Quart. 3 | -0.507 ** | -5.236 | -0.240 ** | -2.342 | -0.252 ** | -2.024 |
| Village mort. | 5.066 ** | 5.415 | 3.449 ** | 3.745 | 5.677 ** | 5.404 |
| Tigray | -0.391 ** | -3.191 | 0.508 ** | 3.831 | 0.032 | 0.195 |
| South | 0.042 | 0.481 | 0.300 ** | 3.297 | 0.565 ** | 5.156 |
| Quit prob. | 0.003 ** | 4.341 | 0.064 ** | 7.159 | 0.069 ** | 5.952 |
|  | Fourth Birth | | Fifth Birth | | Sixth Birth | |
| Alpha | 2.554 ** | 28.320 | 2.704 ** | 23.576 | 2.534 ** | 18.717 |
| Constant | -5.421 ** | -19.512 | -5.944 ** | -17.795 | -6.224 ** | -15.344 |
| BP Wife | 0.029 | 1.443 | 0.022 ** | 0.704 | -0.042 | -0.746 |
| BP Husband | 0.075 ** | 3.455 | 0.074 ** | 3.772 | 0.075 ** | 3.860 |
| Prev. Duration | 0.190 ** | 5.098 | 0.135 ** | 2.243 | 0.454 ** | 4.982 |
| Died | -0.500 ** | -2.172 | -0.140 | 1.301 | 0.475 | 0.786 |
| Agedifference | -0.034 ** | -3.767 | -0.037 ** | -2.667 | -0.051 ** | -3.181 |
| Educ. wife | 0.483 ** | 2.656 | -0.216 ** | -0.916 | 0.097 | 0.357 |
| Educ. husb. | -0.366 ** | -2.799 | 0.172 | 0.965 | -0.228 | -1.095 |
| Married wife | -0.055 | -0.875 | -0.005 | -0.055 | 0.236 ** | 2.270 |
| Married husb. | -0.053 | -0.843 | -0.003 | -0.031 | 0.238 ** | 2.289 |
| Child. wife | -0.222 ** | -2.801 | 0.248* | 1.798 | -0.163 | -1.102 |
| Child. husb. | -0.146* | -1.917 | -0.081 | -1.012 | 0.023 | 0.247 |
| Older 40 | -1.151 ** | -8.469 | -0.513 ** | -3.128 | -0.952 ** | -4.679 |
| Inc. Quart. 1 | 0.009 | 0.057 | 0.678 ** | 3.091 | 0.118 | 0.443 |
| Inc. Quart. 2 | -0.307 ** | -2.038 | 0.020 | 0.103 | -0.566 ** | -2.428 |
| Inc. Quart. 3 | -0.203 | -1.447 | -0.251 | -1.383 | -0.793 ** | -3.194 |
| Village mort. | -0.225 | -0.178 | 1.447 | 0.900 | -1.255 | -0.635 |
| Tigray | 0.762 ** | 3.984 | 0.990 ** | 4.074 | 0.894 ** | 3.069 |
| South | 0.485 ** | 3.812 | 0.351 ** | 2.069 | 0.024 | 0.114 |
| Quit prob. | 0.146 ** | 6.946 | 0.136 ** | 5.495 | 0.106 ** | 6.820 |
| Log-likelihood | -3582.8 | | | | | |
| No. of observations: | 834 | | | | | |

** parameter significant at 5 percent level
* parameter significant at 10 percent level

Bargaining over Fertility 57

Table 12: Jointly estimated parameters of all parities and quit probabilities after third birth

|  | Param. | t-value | Param. | t-value | Param. | t-value |
|---|---|---|---|---|---|---|
|  | First Birth | | Second Birth | | Third Birth | |
| Alpha | 2.262 ** | 38.864 | 2.276 ** | 48.983 | 2.276 ** | 44.248 |
| Constant | −6.157 ** | −34.541 | −5.733 ** | −33.560 | −5.131 ** | −29.098 |
| BP Wife | 0.060 ** | 7.435 | 0.044 ** | 3.553 | 0.003 | 0.330 |
| BP Husband | −0.004 | −0.196 | 0.106 ** | 5.334 | 0.177 ** | 10.802 |
| Prev. Duration |  |  | 0.121 ** | 15.965 | 0.019 | 0.912 |
| Died | −0.659 ** | −8.889 | −1.202 ** | −11.854 | −1.326 ** | −8.459 |
| Agedifference | 0.023 ** | 5.735 | −0.020 ** | −3.849 | −0.051 ** | −6.464 |
| Education wife | −0.209 ** | −2.158 | 0.580 ** | 6.070 | 0.490 ** | 3.668 |
| Education husband | 0.246 ** | 3.304 | −0.142* | −1.702 | −0.716 ** | −7.471 |
| Wife's prev. married | −0.194 ** | −5.022 | 0.095 ** | 2.228 | 0.064 | 1.270 |
| Husband prev. married | −0.192 ** | −4.971 | 0.097 ** | 2.275 | 0.066 | 1.310 |
| Wife's prev. child. | −0.142 ** | −4.061 | −0.174 ** | −4.261 | 0.322 ** | 5.241 |
| Husband's prev. child. | −0.028 | −0.615 | −0.002 | −0.052 | −0.099 ** | −2.021 |
| Older 40 | −1.302 ** | −17.061 | −1.141 ** | −11.911 | −0.794 ** | −7.307 |
| Inc. Quart. 1 | −0.011 | −0.119 | 0.127 | 1.128 | 0.034 | 0.246 |
| Inc. Quart. 2 | −0.187 ** | −2.170 | −0.148 | −1.514 | −0.186 | −1.504 |
| Inc. Quart. 3 | −0.439 ** | −5.377 | −0.175* | −1.859 | −0.192* | −1.692 |
| Village mort. | 5.384 ** | 8.078 | 3.279 ** | 3.835 | 5.885 ** | 6.714 |
| Tigray | −0.387 ** | −3.763 | 0.534 ** | 5.065 | 0.023 | 0.150 |
| South | 0.026 | 0.330 | 0.263 ** | 3.031 | 0.527 ** | 4.857 |
| Quit prob. | 0.004 ** | 4.010 | 0.064 ** | 7.232 | 0.070 ** | 6.117 |
|  | Fourth Birth | | Fifth Birth | | Sixth Birth | |
| Alpha | 2.663 ** | 31.155 | 2.719 ** | 24.540 | 2.514 ** | 20.422 |
| Constant | −6.818 ** | −25.709 | −6.615 ** | −21.145 | −6.794 ** | −18.410 |
| BP Wife | 0.035 ** | 3.308 | 0.080 ** | 2.365 | −0.045 | −1.212 |
| BP Husband | 0.078 ** | 4.627 | 0.066 ** | 3.420 | 0.080 ** | 5.903 |
| Prev. Duration | 0.344 ** | 9.749 | 0.212 ** | 3.168 | 0.475 ** | 5.836 |
| Died | −0.786 ** | −5.813 |  |  | 0.327 | 1.017 |
| Agedifference | −0.028 ** | −3.568 | −0.007 | −0.469 | −0.039 ** | −2.663 |
| Education wife | 0.684 ** | 3.750 | −0.278 | −1.481 | 0.175 | 0.622 |
| Education husband | −0.356 ** | −2.656 | 0.347 ** | 2.120 | −0.154 | −0.917 |
| Wife's prev. married | −0.043 | −0.820 | 0.004 | 0.059 | 0.159* | 1.828 |
| Husband prev. married | −0.041 | −0.782 | 0.006 | 0.088 | 0.161* | 1.851 |
| Wife's prev. child. | −0.226 ** | −2.945 | 0.211 ** | 2.125 | −0.175 | −1.132 |
| Husband's prev. child. | 0.007 | 0.107 | −0.100 | −1.475 | 0.038 | 0.466 |
| Older 40 | −1.231 ** | −10.112 | −0.657 ** | −4.405 | −0.915 ** | −5.067 |
| Inc. Quart. 1 | 0.290 ** | 1.997 | 0.675 ** | 2.917 | 0.313 | 1.350 |
| Inc. Quart. 2 | −0.148 | −1.105 | 0.190 | 1.125 | −0.432 ** | −2.028 |
| Inc. Quart. 3 | 0.076 | 0.623 | −0.038 | −0.205 | −0.453 ** | −2.066 |
| Village mort. | 2.984 ** | 2.848 | 0.158 | 0.124 | −1.327 | −0.801 |
| Tigray | 0.799 ** | 4.451 | 0.972 ** | 4.956 | 0.958 ** | 4.353 |
| South | 0.455 ** | 4.087 | 0.247* | 1.653 | 0.095 | 0.509 |
| Quit prob. | 0.112 ** | 7.103 | 0.142 ** | 5.447 | 0.141 ** | 5.192 |

—— Table continued on next page ——

— Table continued from previous page —

|  | Param. | t-value | Param. | t-value | Param. | t-value |
|---|---|---|---|---|---|---|
|  | Third Birth | | Fourth Birth | | Sixth Birth | |
| Constant | −7.887 ** | −6.194 | −5.045 ** | −6.502 | −17.710 | −22.687 |
| BP Wife | 0.068 | 1.400 | 0.163* | 1.921 | 3.826 | 0.973 |
| BP Husband | 0.096 | 1.426 | −0.278 ** | −2.256 | 0.019 | 0.137 |
| Prev. Duration | 0.328 ** | 3.387 | 0.442 ** | 4.098 | 0.104 | 0.514 |
| Died | −12.031 | −1.127 |  |  | −0.121* | −1.662 |
| Agedifference | 0.054* | 1.816 | −1.664 | −1.085 | −9.472 ** | −3.022 |
| Education wife | −14.527 | −0.950 | 0.128 ** | 4.703 | −1.553 | −1.255 |
| Education husband | 0.542 | 1.145 | −16.617 | −0.832 | −0.878* | −1.833 |
| Wife's prev. married | 0.461* | 1.714 | 1.793 ** | 3.584 | −0.876* | −1.829 |
| Husband prev. married | 0.463* | 1.721 | 0.712 ** | 2.741 | 0.053 | 0.132 |
| Wife's prev. child. | −0.270 | −1.346 | 0.714* | 2.749 | −0.085 | −0.262 |
| Husband's prev. child. | 0.186 | 1.377 | 0.294 | 1.367 | 15.787 ** | 11.057 |
| Older 40 | 2.830 ** | 3.012 | −0.819 ** | −2.630 | 3.216 ** | 2.562 |
| Inc. Quart. 1 | −0.155 | −0.343 | 0.200 | 0.442 | 2.444* | 1.966 |
| Inc. Quart. 2 | 0.591 | 0.992 | 0.729 | 0.962 | 2.912 ** | 2.336 |
| Inc. Quart. 3 | −0.033 | −0.069 | 0.685 | 0.801 | 11.000 | 1.290 |
| Village mort. | 2.953 | 0.791 | 0.863 | 1.195 | −3.876 ** | −2.452 |
| Tigray | 0.056 | 0.095 | −20.783 ** | −4.189 | −1.531* | −1.658 |
| South | −0.819 | −1.571 | 0.204 | 0.190 | −0.574 | −1.060 |
| Log-likelihood |  | −7574.7 |  |  |  |  |
| No. of observations: |  | 834 |  |  |  |  |

** parameter significant at 5 percent level
* parameter significant at 10 percent level

# Bargaining over Fertility

## Table 13: Poisson model

| | Parameters | t-values |
|---|---|---|
| BP Wife | −0.192 ** | −2.797 |
| BP Husband | 0.017 ** | 2.661 |
| Age difference | −0.005 | −0.814 |
| Prim. school. husband | 0.099 | 0.778 |
| Prev. relations wife | 0.032 | 0.184 |
| Previous relation husband | −0.256 | −1.464 |
| Prev. child. Wife | 0.046 | 0.640 |
| Prev. child. Husband | −0.115 ** | −2.129 |
| Age of woman | −0.022 ** | −3.512 |
| Inc. Quart. 1 | −0.192 | −1.532 |
| Inc. Quart. 2 | −0.165 | −1.327 |
| Inc. Quart. 3 | −0.310 ** | −2.285 |
| Village mortality | 2.691 * | 1.820 |
| Tigray | 0.043 | 0.301 |
| South | 0.341 ** | 2.776 |
| Constant | 2.655 ** | 6.878 |
| Log-Likelihood | 285.781 | |
| LR-$\chi_1^2$ | 86.572 | p: 0.000 |
| Akaike | −539.562 | |

** significant at 5 percent level
* significant at 10 percent level

## Table 14: Negative binomial model

| | Parameters | t-values |
|---|---|---|
| BP Wife | −0.193 ** | −2.594 |
| BP Husband | 0.016 ** | 2.168 |
| Age difference | −0.005 | −0.625 |
| Prim. school. husband | 0.125 | 0.786 |
| Prev. relations wife | 0.035 | 0.175 |
| Previous relation husband | −0.267 | −1.296 |
| Prev. child. Wife | 0.045 | 0.554 |
| Prev. child. Husband | −0.121 ** | −1.985 |
| Age of woman | −0.024 ** | −3.240 |
| Inc. Quart. 1 | −0.215 | −1.410 |
| Inc. Quart. 2 | −0.199 | −1.307 |
| Inc. Quart. 3 | −0.333 ** | −2.050 |
| Village mortality | 2.991 * | 1.669 |
| Tigray | 0.021 | 0.124 |
| South | 0.365 ** | 2.468 |
| Constant | 2.763 ** | 5.927 |
| $\alpha$ | 0.089 ** | 2.023 |
| Log-Likelihood | 264.73529 | |
| LR-$\chi_1^2$ | 56.117 | p: 0.000 |
| Akaike | −538.341 | |

** significant at 5 percent level
* significant at 10 percent level

Table 15: Two-component count model of no. of child

|  | Component 1 | | Component 2 | |
| --- | --- | --- | --- | --- |
|  | Parameter | t-values | Parameter | t-values |
| BP Wife | −0.450 ** | −1.925 | −0.182 ** | −2.157 |
| BP Husband | 0.045 ** | 3.771 | 0.015* | 1.876 |
| Age difference | 0.005 | 0.411 | −0.007 | −0.872 |
| Prim. school. husband | 0.259 | 1.155 | −0.293 | −1.545 |
| Prev. relations wife | 1.597 ** | 3.042 | −0.067 | −0.347 |
| Previous relation husband | −2.233 ** | −3.755 | −0.050 | −0.259 |
| Prev. child. Wife | 0.493 ** | 2.470 | 0.014 | 0.169 |
| Prev. child. Husband | 0.261 ** | 2.338 | −0.169 ** | −2.499 |
| Age of woman | 0.003 | 0.323 | −0.062 ** | −5.974 |
| Inc. Quart. 1 | −0.181 | −0.678 | 0.089 | 0.587 |
| Inc. Quart. 2 | 0.411* | 1.767 | −0.293* | −1.808 |
| Inc. Quart. 3 | 0.060 | 0.214 | −0.248 | −1.524 |
| Village mortality | −6.397* | −1.754 | 3.670* | 1.913 |
| Tigray | 1.064 ** | 3.128 | −0.189 | −1.094 |
| South | 1.212 ** | 4.086 | 0.118 | 0.770 |
| Constant | 0.351 | 0.452 | 4.789 ** | 8.266 |
| Component probabilities | 0.301 | | 0.699 | |
| Log-likelihood: | 331.707 | | | |
| LR-$\chi_1^2$ | 178.424 | p: 0.000 | | |
| Akaike: one component | | −539.562 | | |
| Akaike: two components | | −599.414 | | |

** significant at 5 percent level
* significant at 10 percent level

# 4 Patterns of consumption and child welfare in female headed households in Tanzania

## 4.4 Introduction

This paper is concerned with patterns of expenditure and child welfare among male headed (MHH) and female headed households (FHH) in Tanzania. It is often argued that women do care more about children than men and thus such behavior should be reflected by household expenditure within MHH and FHH.[24] I estimate Engel curves to investigate household expenditure patterns while controlling for household characteristics and find that FHH spend significantly more money on the welfare of children and less on consumption of adult goods.[25] Welfare of children is defined here in a narrow sense and measured by the response of household demand to changes in household demographic composition for food, child clothing and education. Alcohol and tobacco are treated as adult goods as they are assumed to be entirely consumed by adults. The study further explores the reasons for such different spending patterns. One explanation is offered by the old-age security hypothesis which states that persons lacking the financial means to rely on themselves during old-age invest more in children who care for them. Women might be more constrained in terms of financial resources, assets and access to financial institutions and therefore invest more in children. The findings on the empirical content of the old-age security hypothesis are mixed and do not unambiguously support the old-age hypothesis.

The distribution of resources within households has received wide attention in the past which has been spurred with the works of Manser and Brown (1980), McElroy and Horney (1981), Chiappori (1992), and Browning and Chiappori (1998). In these models, individuals are assumed to form a household while retaining their own personal interests and bargain with other members to accomplish their goals. The control over resources, individual contribution to household welfare or social status which are associated with bargaining power define the extent to which an individual can affect household decision making. The more bargaining power, the more say an individual has. In response to these considerations, a number of empirical papers are concerned with the question of the impact of women's bargaining power on household decision making. The empirical studies often find that the food share tends to increase with increasing status of women (see Quisumbing and Maluccio 2000, Haddad and Hoddinott 1994, Thomas 1990, Thomas 1993).

---

[24] See Haddad (1999) for a summary and further references.

[25] I consider tobacco and alcohol as adult goods in line with foregoing studies that have demonstrated the demographic separability of these items. Demographic separability implies that increasing consumption of these items only leads to an income effect, but do not bring about substitution of expenditure from an adult good toward a child good as clothing for children (Deaton, Ruiz-Castillo and Thomas 1989).

Extending this idea to the welfare of children, others have looked at the impact of women's bargaining position on the nutritional status of children or the household's expenditure on education (Thomas 1994, Thomas, Lavy and Strauss 1996, Thomas and Strauss 1992). The general result of these papers is that women seem to care more for children, which finds its expression expenditure shares for child goods which rise with improvements of the status of women. The measurement of female status is however difficult and subject to discussion. The first problem relates to the operationalization of status. First, one may consider status in economic terms, that is, women who contribute substantial income to the household should be regarded as having more say in household decision making. But status may also be defined by cultural norms which assign women a particular role that determines their influence on decisions. Finally, personality affects the position women occupy within the household. While the latter two are difficult to measure, most studies rely on economic variables. Individual contribution may be expressed through cash income earned on the wage labor market, cash transfers which are tied to a person or simply assets which can be sold or used for the production of goods. This approach not only neglects the value of household work—which may be or may be not perceived as economically valuable by household members—but is also particularly troublesome in agrarian and subsistence dominated societies where wage labor is not wide spread or almost non-existent. Income based measures are furthermore subject to endogeneity problems, since the decision to work is a function of bargaining power. That is, individuals with a larger say—because of personality or other characteristics—may decide not to work at all. Personality is unobserved which why income as a measure of bargaining power is potentially correlated with the error term. A solution might be to use control over assets. However, the same problem arises from assets purchased during marriage which why many studies employ assets brought to marriage which are independent from current decision making and personality effects. However, all these measures are subject to measurement error and it is still unclear to what extent they really reflect true individual bargaining power.

In view of these difficulties, it is desirable to find other ways to isolate female and male influence on household decision making. One option is to compare MHH and FHH and to assume that headship reflects decision making power. This approach is not entirely free of problems. It assumes first that FHH are a homogeneous group which is not the case in Tanzania and many other sub-Saharan African countries (see discussion in chapter 2). A FHH may arise out of widowhood or divorce whereas in other cases women are married but the husband has temporarily outmigrated. However, in those households where no male partner is present which is due for most FHH in Tanzania which consist of either divorced or widowed women, men are unlikely to exert a major influence on how consumption expenditure is to be used and how much money is allocated to it.[26] Although the estimates might be slightly biased due to the identification problem of the true household decision maker, it should be still possible to estimate average effects and to investigate these for systematic differences between FHH and MHH.

A common approach to compare expenditure patterns of FHH and MHH is to introduce a dummy variable representing the sex of the household head. This approach assumes a linear. that is, parallel scaling of the demand curves in response to the household head's sex. The results presented here show that this assumption does not hold for some goods. Furthermore, by applying the dummy variable approach it is not possible to investigate different responses of expenditure behavior to an additional child in different age and sex groups as well as the impact of the household head's education and sex. Some studies do not embed their analysis in a demand framework or ignore the fact that a number of goods exhibit zero expenditures. Others do not consider control variables as demographic composition of the household. The approach followed here is to estimate Engel curves separately for each household category and to compare the parameters and the resulting curves in order to trace different expenditure patterns. Furthermore, I estimate expenditure elasticities for each household category to investigate how demand responds to changes in total consumption.

## 4.4 The old-age security motive for investing in children

The evidence to date that FHH spend more on child welfare is mixed. Some studies using African data demonstrate a positive impact of female headship on child welfare (Bruce 1989, Kennedy and Peters 1992). Handa (1994, 1996a) repeats this result for the case of Jamaica while Rogers (1995) finds that among MHH and FHH in The Dominican Republic, there are no substantial differences in the level of food demand while controlling for household characteristics and food prices. However, children in FHH at the lowest range of income on the other hand tend to be better nourished compared to MHH.

Empirical papers on female spending on child welfare yet largely do not attempt to explain this empirical regularity. Many authors attribute this to the fact that mothers are closer to their children through household chores and child care in general which is seen as a women's task rendering women more aware of their children's well-being (Bruce 1989, Rogers 1995, Handa 1996a). Haddad (1999) lists some further conjectures: (i) women may be driven by social and cultural norms to ensure an adequate share of food for children. (ii) Women spend more time with their children and thus have naturally a closer relation to them, which induces women to spend more on child welfare. (iii) Due to time constraints, women in FHH may also buy more processed food which is more expensive but

---

[26]This is not true regarding consumption expenditures. See subsequent chapter on FHH and production efficiency.

easier to prepare. (iv) The general longer life expectancy of women and the risk of divorce and widowhood induces women to invest more in the health of their children. Due to biological reasons the life expectancy is higher for women as compared to men and therefore women can be expected to outlive their husbands. Women are also often married to older men, which further increases the risk of being widowed at early ages. In case of widowhood, poor women need help from their children to ensure survival.

The 'investment in children' argument for securing support from children during old ages comes close to the old-age security explanation for fertility. The claim that couples use children as a risk coping strategy has found some empirical support by Cain (1981, 1983) and Nugent and Gillaspy (1983). In an early review of the old-age security motive of couples in developing countries to get children Nugent (1985) illustrates the different underlying conditions for which the motive may hold and outlines 8 different causes: (i) underdeveloped capital markets, (ii) uncertainty about the quantity of marketable goods and financial assets necessary as insurance for old age and disability, (iii) absence of inefficient insurance programs, (iv) loyalty of children to their parents, (v) absence of markets for labor that allow women to generate income, (vi) underdeveloped markets for goods and services that elderly people consume, (vii) absence of a young spouse, and finally (viii) the perception of the relative importance of old age. The first three points refer to the existence and functioning of capital and insurance markets and the perceptions about the importance and possibility to access them. The fourth point refers to social norms, which in developing countries often ensure respect and loyalty of children to their parents. In the past, such loyalty might have decreased due to migration and abating social control. However, parents, who complain about the lack of loyalty they receive from their children, may simply want to extract more services from them (Nugent 1985). The capability to accumulate assets for the purpose of old age security depends on the possibility to produce sufficient surplus that can be saved. Self-employment is often considered as a survival strategy and most farming systems hardly satisfy subsistence requirements. Saving is therefore often dependent on the functioning of labor markets, which are often restricted and underdeveloped in developing countries. As the data from the Tanzanian Integrated Labor Force Survey (URT (2002)) show, only 4.0 percent of economically active women find wage employment as opposed to 9.8 percent of the working male population. The seventh point refers particularly to women, since it is common in Tanzania and other developing countries that women are younger than their husbands. Older men on the other hand often receive support by their younger wives as has been noted by Cain (1982).

The points made by Nugent and others may not be restricted to fertility but might also apply to investments in child quality. Where the likelihood to become a widow at early ages is large and where means of insurance are lacking, women have an incentive to invest in the wellbeing and education of their children to ensure their support during old age. In this regard, wellbeing of children is a function of the expectations of the mother that her children will support her in old age. When an individual has no means to save, then investment into the human capital of children—that is health and education of the children—increases the returns during old age. This may hold particularly in cases where women cannot re-marry or are too old to get further children. When replacing fertility with child quality—where quality refers to health and education—then child quality and savings should appear as substitutes if the old-age security hypothesis is correct.[27] At the core of the test proposed here is the introduction of savings into the demand function for child goods and food. I focus here only on food which can be regarded as investment into child health and education which is the most direct translation of spending on children into future human capital of children.

## 4.4 The data

Tanzania makes a good case for the comparison of MHH and FHH as the incidence of FHH is quite large like in many other sub-Saharan African countries. The data is taken from the Tanzanian Household Budget Survey 2000/01 which covers all 20 mainland regions. After cleaning the sample consists of 18,783 households out of which 4,737 households classify themselves as FHH which amounts to a share of 25.2 percent. Although this is a large number, it is not unusual for sub-Saharan countries.

The expenditure items covered are food, education[28] and child clothing as child goods and alcohol and tobacco as adult goods. The treatment of food as a child good is strictly speaking not correct. However, as the food shares increase, it is likely that child nutrition or their share in food consumption increases as well. To what extent it changes, is subject of investigation in this study. Household demographics are included in the demand equations as well and are captured by the log of total household size and by the share of individuals in different age and gender categories relative to household size. Summary statistics of the data are given in table 16. Food is the major expenditure item of Tanzanian households and amounts to more than 60 percent for both household categories. The averages do not differ substantially between household categories; the expenditure shares for food in FHH are on average 3 percentage points higher compared to MHH. FHH spend also more on education and child clothing as reflected by the statistics, but again the means do not differ to a large extent. Expenditure on alcohol is very low which is partly due to low prices for alcohol. Tobacco expenditures are higher but do not exceed 5 percent on average. For both adult good categories, the shares are lower among FHH.

---

[27]This argument has also been put forward by Cigno (1993).

[28]It should be noted that the data was collected before the abandonment of school fees for primary schools was implemented in 2003.

FHH tend to be smaller and as to be expected exhibit a low share of male adults and a high share of female adults. Otherwise, the household demographic composition does not reveal significant differences between household categories. Education of the head of household is included to approximate different types of work as it can be assumed that farmers and workers have different food needs compared to white collar workers. Furthermore, education may imply different preferences to certain goods. It is notable that the average educational level of the head of household in FHH is substantially below the level of MHH. Only 39 percent of female heads are primary educated and less than 10 percent have achieved secondary education. The availability of land is also lower in FHH compared to MHH as well as the number of existing savings accounts. The reported averages need to be interpreted in the light of lower expenditure propensities among FHH for adult goods. As shown in table 17, the number of FHH that purchase adult goods at all is smaller. Only 20 percent of FHH spend money on alcohol as opposed to 30 percent in MHH. Regarding tobacco, almost twice as much MHH purchase cigarettes or related products, while only 16 percent of FHH do so. Consumption of tobacco is probably also culturally determined, as women are not supposed to smoke, particularly so among muslims. Slightly more FHH have purchased child clothing, while the shares for education are almost the same.

## 4.4 Comparison of regression curves

### 4.4.1 Empirical approach

To compare demand behavior across household categories, I begin with estimating for each household category $j$ and good $k$ separately a simple model of the form

$$w_{ijk} = m(\ln(x_{ij})) + \alpha z_{ij} + \beta d_{ij} + \varepsilon_{ijk} \qquad (34)$$

where $z_{ij}$ is a vector of variables that capture the demographic profile of the $i$th household of category $j$, $n$ is household size and $d$ denotes a set of regional dummy variables.[29] Finally, the model includes controls for the 20 Tanzanian regions[30] as well as a dummy for rural households. The functional relationship between expenditure shares $w$ and the log of total expenditure per capita $\ln x$ is left unspecified which bears several advantages. First, this model is theoretically consistent as has been shown by Blundell, Duncan and Pendakur (1998) and exhibits all features of a well behaved demand function. Second, it has been found for the case of developing countries that models linear in the logarithm of total expenditure are not appropriate because Engel curves based on logarithmic expenditure are often non-linear. In developing countries food Engel curves tend to be quadratic (see Bhalotra and Attfield 1998, Deaton and Paxson 1998). Even a

---
[29]This model can be directly derived from an indirect utility function. (see Pendakur 1999).
[30]Zansibar is not included in the HBS data.

quadratic form may be overly restrictive as it is plausible that with rising incomes, poor people substitute high quality food for lower quality food, which would cause the Engel curve to be flat (or with an upward trend) at the lowest range of expenditures. The more income is available, the steeper the downward slope of the curve may get, while flattening out at the higher income ranges. Such a cubic trend is likely for countries exhibiting high levels of income inequality and severe poverty, although violating Gorman's (1981) rank three condition for exactly aggregable demand systems.[31]

The function $m(\cdot)$ and parameters $\alpha$ and $\beta$ are obtained by applying the partial linear model proposed by Robinson (1988) and Speckman (1988). Denoting $z = (z, d)$ and $\beta = (\alpha, \beta)$ one may write (34) in the general form

$$w = m(x) + z\beta + u \qquad (35)$$

and obtain the parameter vector $\beta$ through

$$\hat{\beta} = \left[(z - \hat{m}(z \mid x))(z - \hat{m}(z \mid x))'\right]^{-1}\left[(z - \hat{m}(z \mid x))(y - \hat{m}(y \mid x))\right] \qquad (36)$$

where $m(z \mid x)$ denotes the nonparametric first moment of $z$ conditional on $x$. The standard errors of $\hat{\beta}$ are calculated using the sandwich estimator $\Phi^{-1}\Xi\Phi^{-1}$, where $\Phi = N^{-1}\sum_i(x_i - \hat{m}(z_i \mid x_i))(x - \hat{m}(z_i \mid x_i)')]$ and $\Xi = N^{-1}\sum_i(x_i - \hat{m}(z_i \mid x_i))(x - \hat{m}(z_i \mid x_i)'\varepsilon_i^2$. The nonparametric curve given by $m(x)$ can be recovered by regressing $w - z\beta$ on $x$.

The nonparametric part of the model is estimated using a weighted local polynomial regression (LOWESS) smoother which has been proposed by Cleveland (1979). Each point of the smoothed curve is calculated by

$$m(x) = \sum_i^N (y_i - \alpha_p - \beta_p(x_i - x))^2 K\left(\frac{x_i - x}{h}\right) \qquad (37)$$

where (37) is minimized with respect to $\alpha_p$ and $\beta_p$. The function $K(\cdot)$ denotes a Kernel density with bandwidth $h$. The bandwidth is chosen via generalized cross-validation which involves minimizing the criterion

$$GCV = \frac{\sum \varepsilon^2}{(1 - n^{-1}\text{tr}(S))} \qquad (38)$$

where $\varepsilon$ denotes the residuals obtained from (37) and $S$ is the smoothing matrix (Ruppert, Wand and Carroll 2003). Further, I provide estimates of the confidence

---

[31]Gorman (1981) has shown that any exactly aggregable demand system that satisfies utility maximization is at most of rank three, implying that a cubic term of the log of expenditure does not generate any additional informational gains.

intervals of the curves based on the smooth conditional moment (SCM) method suggested by Gozalo (1997). An advantage of this method as opposed to the wild bootstrap is that it is not only robust to heteroscedasticity, but also to violations of the normality assumption of the residuals. Although the LOWESS estimator exhibits better end effects as Nadaraya-Watson or Spline estimators it is not entirely immune to outliers in regions where data are sparse and hence the data have been trimmed by dropping the upper and lower 2.5% quantiles from the sample.

The estimation of the parameters using (34) is made difficult by two problems: (i) endogeneity bias due to the construction of the independent variable and (ii) endogeneity bias arising from the censoring of the dependent variable for all goods except food.

The theory of two-stage budgeting suggests that households divide the available budget into expenditure and savings and then decide on which goods to buy. Hence, total expenditure is a choice variable not exogenous to the consumer. Furthermore, the budget shares are calculated by dividing outlay for the $k$th good by total expenditure. But the measurement of household expenditure in developing countries is generally plagued by a number of difficulties like seasonal variation, recall errors, etc., which render expenditure data imprecise. Since the budget shares are constructed by dividing expenditure on the $k$th good by total expenditure, the measurement error found in expenditure must translate into a measurement error of the budget share. Consequently, the independent variable household expenditure is correlated with the error term. Hausman (1978) has derived a regression based test for endogeneity. The same framework can also be applied to account for inconsistency of the parameter estimates in the presence of endogeneity bias. The test as discussed in Hausman's paper is originally based on purely parametric methods but extends to and has found applications in the semiparametric framework as well.[32] Consider the following model

$$E(w_i \mid x_i, z_i) = m(x_i) + \beta z_i + u_i \qquad (39)$$

where $x$ is correlated with error term $u$, $m(\cdot)$ is again an undefined function and $z$ is a matrix containing variables which are assumed to be strictly exogenous. To conduct the test, assume that an instrumental variable $y$ highly correlated with $x$ but not correlated with $u$ is available and regress $x$ on $y$ as well as on the exogenous variables contained in $z$ and obtain $\nu$ given by the model

$$E(x_i \mid y_i, z_i) = \lambda y_i + \gamma z_i + \nu_i \qquad (40)$$

Running regression (40) yields an estimate $\hat{\nu}_i$ which is introduced into (39)

$$w_i = m(x_i) + \beta z_i + \delta \hat{\nu}_i + \varepsilon_i \qquad (41)$$

---

[32]See Blundell et al. (1998) for an application.

If $\delta$ in equation 41 turns out to be significantly different from zero, the null of no endogeneity bias present in the model must be rejected. Hausman demonstrates, that the inclusion of $\hat{\nu}$ is suited to yield consistent estimates of $\alpha$ and $\beta$ which in turn produce a consistent estimate of the nonparametric part of the model.

The problem of dealing with endogeneity of this form is the availability of instruments for expenditure. A frequently used variable is the log of total income per capita, which is just as problematic as total per capita consumption. Income fluctuates substantially in developing countries which leads many poor households to smooth consumption over time. High levels of income are therefore not indicative of high levels of expenditure. Furthermore, income is subject to even larger measurement problems as in the HBS it is recorded on the basis of a one year recall. The survey also contains a component that collects income data on a monthly basis, but given the seasonal fluctuation of income–which holds for agricultural income as well as for wage labor which is often not permanent–this only partially solves the problem. The problem to measure income accurately implies that income is a weak instrument for expenditure in the present setting. Weak instruments, however, lead to large standard errors of the instrumented variable rendering statistical inference difficult. Furthermore, if a weak instrument is even slightly correlated with the error term, then instrumental variable regression yields severely biased results which does not even disappear asymptotically (see Wooldridge (2002) for a discussion of this issue).

Expenditure on the other hand is much more stable over time and is recorded at a higher frequency and covers an entire month.[33] The measurement error of consumption is therefore probably lower as compared to income. Given that the correlation between log of income per capita and log of expenditure per capita amounts to only 0.25 and that the impact of a weak instrument can be much more severe than the actual bias from not employing any instrument, the reported parameters in the tables are not corrected for endogeneity bias of this type as further suitable instruments are not available. When using income as an instrument for expenditure and including $\hat{\nu}$ in the set of equations, $\hat{\delta}$ turns out to be significant in most cases. However, the resulting estimates and the demand curves become unreasonable as the predicted expenditure shares are not anymore bounded between zero and one. Previous studies using income as an instrument for expenditure in a developed country context where data quality is much better demonstrate that the impact of endogeneity bias on the actual parameters is quite weak. However, the expected improvement of the quality of the estimates obtained here is probably low, even if suitable instruments were available (e.g., Blundell et al. 1998).

The second source of endogeneity bias arises from the censoring of the dependent variable for all non-food goods. In order to account for this problem I

---

[33]Enumerators have visited the households at least 8 times over one month and collected data on consumption items.

adapt a two-stage estimation procedure of a generalized Tobit model for the semi-parametric framework (see for expositions of the approach for purely parametric models Amemiya 1985, Cragg 1971, Maddala 1983).[34] First redefine (34) as a latent variable model that describes demand for the $i$th good

$$w_{ijk} = \begin{cases} f(x_{ij}) + \alpha z_{ij} + \beta d_{ij} + \varepsilon_{ijk} & \text{if } w_{ijk}^* > 0 \\ 0 & \text{otherwise} \end{cases} \quad (42)$$

The latent variable $w_{ijk}^*$ is defined by

$$w_{ijk}^* = \gamma x_{ij} + \alpha z_{ij} + \beta d_{ij} + \kappa_{ijk} \quad (43)$$

and determines whether the $j$th good is chosen or not. That is, if $w_{ijk}^*$ exceeds zero, the household decides to purchase the good. Unfortunately, $w_{ijk}^*$ is unobserved but its sign can be recovered from whether the household buys the good or not. If the good is purchased, then $w_{ijk}^*$ is positive and negative otherwise. Now assume that

$$\begin{pmatrix} \varepsilon_{ijk} \\ \kappa_{ijk} \end{pmatrix} \sim N \left[ \begin{pmatrix} 0 \\ 0 \end{pmatrix}, \begin{pmatrix} \sigma_1^2 & \rho\sigma_1 \\ \rho\sigma_1 & 1 \end{pmatrix} \right] \quad (44)$$

Using $\mathbf{X}\gamma$ as a shortcut for the parameters and independent variables involved in (43) along with the conditional first moment of a bivariate truncated normal distribution, yields the conditional expectation

$$E(w_{ijk} \mid w_{ijk} > 0) = f(x_{ij}) + \alpha z_{ij} + \beta d_{ij} + \sigma \frac{\phi_{ij}(\mathbf{X}\gamma)}{\Phi_{ij}(\mathbf{X}\gamma)} \quad (45)$$

where $\phi_{ij}(\cdot)$ and $\Phi_{ij}(\cdot)$ denote the standard normal density and distribution functions, respectively. This model can be estimated by applying Heckman's two-step approach (Heckman 1976), where initial parameters for $\gamma$ are estimated in a first stage probit model with

$$I_i = 1 \quad \text{if } w_{ijk} > 0 \quad (46)$$
$$I_i = 0 \quad \text{otherwise} \quad (47)$$

as the dependent variable. Using the estimates $\hat{\gamma}$, the inverse Mills ratio $\hat{\phi}_i/\hat{\Phi}_i$ is constructed and substituted into (45), which can now be estimated using any consistent estimation procedure. Note, that the method explicitly allows the log of expenditure per capita to enter the first stage probit model parametrically instead of in a non-parametric form.[35]

---

[34]Two-step methods for censored models based on the inverse Mills ratio have been criticized for being inconsistent and not utilizing the full sample in the second (see Shonkwiler and Yen 1999). However, the alternative two-step method proposed by Shonkwiler and Yen exhibits inferior behavior compared to Heckman approaches when the extent of censoring exceeds 50 percent (Tauchmann 2005).

[35]Each probit equation has been tested for the inclusion of a squared term of expenditure per capita. The results of test are given along with the estimated parameters.

The two-step procedure is subject to heteroscedasticity that can be accounted for either through the formula given in Heckman (1979) or by following the suggestion from Amemiya (1985) to estimate the variance-covariance matrix via $\Phi^{-1}\bar{\Xi}\Phi^{-1}$ which is the same as defined above, only that $\varepsilon_{ijk}$ in $\bar{\Xi}$ is replaced by $\bar{\varepsilon}_{ijk} = w_{ijk} - f(x_{ij}) - \alpha z_{ij} - \beta d_{ij} - \sigma\frac{\phi_{ij}(X\gamma)}{\Phi_{ij}(X\gamma)}$. In this study I follow the latter approach since it is easier to compute.

### 4.4.2 Estimates of the Engel curves

Figure 3 shows the food Engel curves for FHH and MHH, respectively. In all figures that follow, the dashed lines around the curves represent the 5 percent confidence intervals. Both curves have the expected downward slope and exhibit an approximately quadratic shape. There is a clear difference between the two curves indicating that food demand is systematically higher in FHH compared to MHH at the same levels of per capita expenditure. The difference amounts to about 6 percentage points at the lower ends of per capita expenditure, to 3 percentage points in the middle and to almost 10 percentage points at the upper consumption range. This difference is remarkable as poorer FHH focus on food more than MHH in either quality or quantity. Given the price levels of basic food as maize and some vegetables in Tanzania a difference of 6 percentage points imply a substantial difference in food consumption among household members in FHH.[36] A further observation worth noting is the fact that the MHH curve first increases until it reaches its saddle point at 10.84 of log expenditure per capita and starts to fall thereafter. The curve for FHH constantly exhibits a negative slope which suggests that among the poorest, FHH tend to assign greater importance to sufficient food supply compared to MHH. The curves further reveal no convergence but rather diverge with increasing expenditure. From an old-age security perspective, FHH therefore appear not to treat children as an investment good, as it may be assumed that savings and capital accumulation increase with rising expenditure levels.

The Engel curves for clothing and education are shown in figures 4 and 5. FHH spend more on child clothing, too. The curve for FHH remains above the MHH's curve across almost the whole range of expenditure. Differences are not substantial but may be overcompensated by better maintenance of child clothing within FHH. Demand for education exhibits the same path within both household categories at the lower end of expenditure but diverges slightly at the upper end.

The curves for the adult goods alcohol and tobacco exhibit substantially different shapes. While expenditure for alcohol is larger among FHH at lower ranges of expenditure the curves eventually cross. The FHH curve for alcohol is almost

---

[36]The mean price for maize grain, which is one of the major food crops and has the richest content of calories among the subsistence crops (on average 368 calories per 100 grams), cost 0.1 US dollar per kg. Sorghum grain which is also consumed in large quantities has similar prices and calorie contents (HBS 2000/01).

**Figure 3: Food budget shares for FHH and MHH**

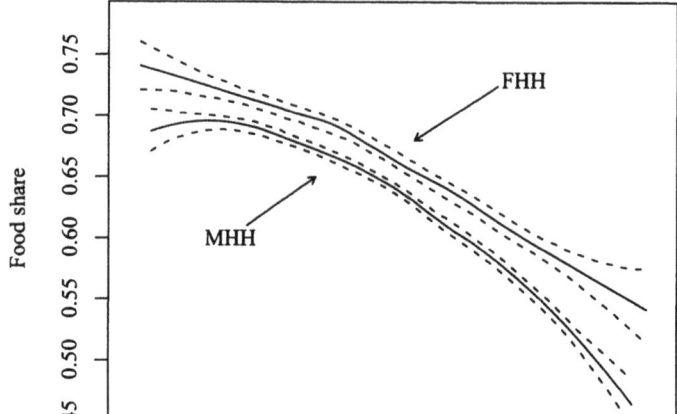

linear and falls over the whole range of expenditure. Alcohol shares in MHH first fall but remain constant at 0.6 percent of total expenditure after crossing the FHH curve. Although FHH exhibit higher alcohol shares among poorer households, the overall budget share for alcoholic beverages does not even exceed 1 percent. However, prices for alcohol are low and consumption is often restricted to local brews as pombe, which can be produced very cheaply. Thus even small amounts of expenditure can imply substantial quantities of consumption. The curves need to be further interpreted in the light of the different consumption propensities of alcohol among FHH and MHH whereas MHH tend to exhibit a higher likelihood of alcohol consumption (see table 17). At the lowest range of expenditure, tobacco shares for FHH amount to 4.4 percent of the budget share while those for MHH start at 5.0 percent. Both curves exhibit on average a negative slope and remain distant from each other, though they do not appear to be parallel.

As a first indication of significance of the distance between the curves one may use the confidence intervals which are given by the dashed lines around the two curves, although, as Härdle, Müller, Sperlich and Werwatz (2004) note, those confidence intervals should not be used for statistical testing of the difference of two curves. The results for all different goods, although less clearly for education, visually establish systematically different patterns of demand for food and child goods as well for the adult goods alcohol and tobacco. Whether this conclusion

Patterns of Demand

Figure 4: Budget shares for clothing in FHH and MHH

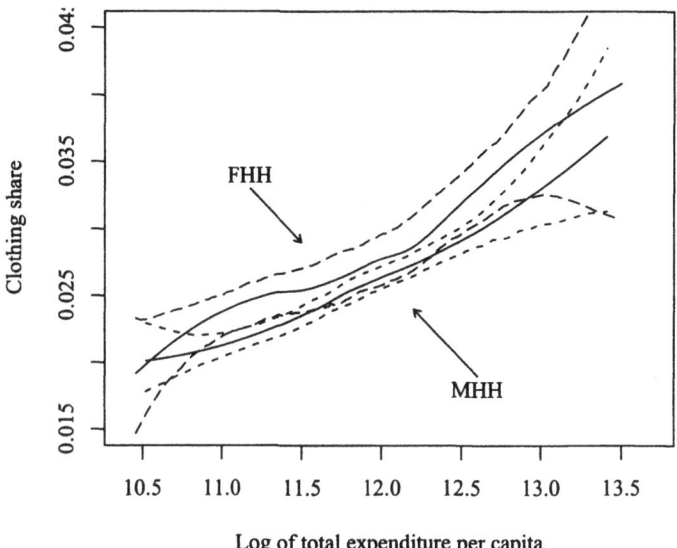

Log of total expenditure per capita

holds after statistical testing is investigated in the following section.

### 4.4.3 Testing for shape equality

Testing the equality of two regression curves is a common problem that is frequently addressed in the literature although most often for fixed design data. The fixed design refers to the case where the range of observations of the independent variable is the same for both curves, which renders such tests more appropriate for the comparison of different independent variables within the same data set. The Tanzanian household data is not conform to a fixed design, since the MHH and FHH data are treated here as two distinct populations with observations randomly distributed along the x-axis, and therefore do not match each other exactly.

The test pursued is based on the ideas of Härdle and Marron (1990) and Yatchew (1999) and (i) can handle random design data and (ii) allows for consecutive testing of two different hypotheses. The first hypothesis arises from the question whether the two curves are significantly distant from each other. To address this problem, one first seeks the set of parameters that most closely translates one curve into the other and check whether these parameters are significantly different from zero. In case the parameters are significant, the difference (or remoteness) of the curves would have been established. The second hypothesis is concerned with the

**Figure 5: Budget shares for education in FHH and MHH**

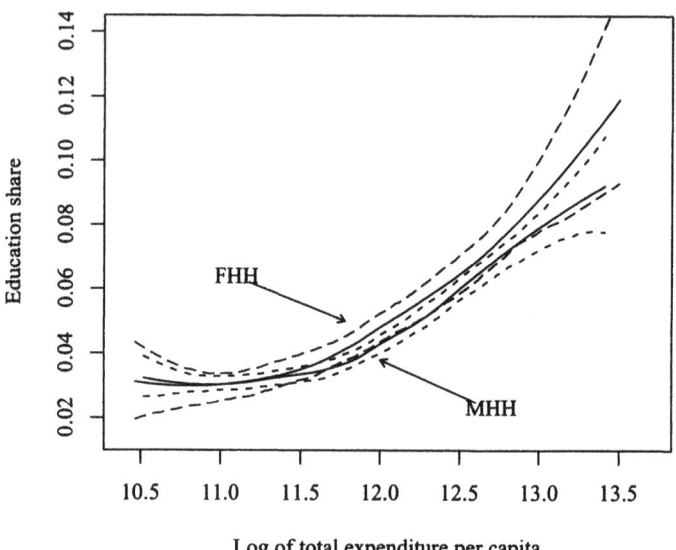

Log of total expenditure per capita

similarity of the shape of the two curves. If both household categories exhibit the same pattern of expenditure for the different goods, although at different levels of expenditure, then the curves should be parallel. The first step of the test involves the estimation of a single index model of the form

$$w_{ij} = m(\ln(x_i) - \delta c_i) + \alpha c_i + \varepsilon_{ij} \qquad (48)$$

where $c$ denotes a dummy variable taking on the value 1 for FHH.[37] The parameter $\delta$ causes a horizontal shift of the curve of FHH toward the MHH curve, while $\alpha$ leads to a vertical scaling. Equation (48) is estimated by applying a method based on differencing, as proposed by Yatchew, Sun and Deri (2003), and which is described in appendix 4.1. The results are presented in Table 18. The estimated scale parameters $\alpha$ shown in the first row are all significant at the 5-percent level thus statistically establishing the vertical distance between the demand curves and confirming the visual difference of the curves. Only the shift parameters $\beta$ presented in the third row of 18 are insignificant for non-food items, but significant for food.

The second part of the test evaluates whether the two regression curves exhibit the same shape. The test proceeds along the lines of the differencing procedure

---
[37] Note that the functional form of (48) does not correspond to the form suggested by Härdle and Marron (1990), but the principle is the same.

## Figure 6: Budget shares for alcohol in FHH and MHH

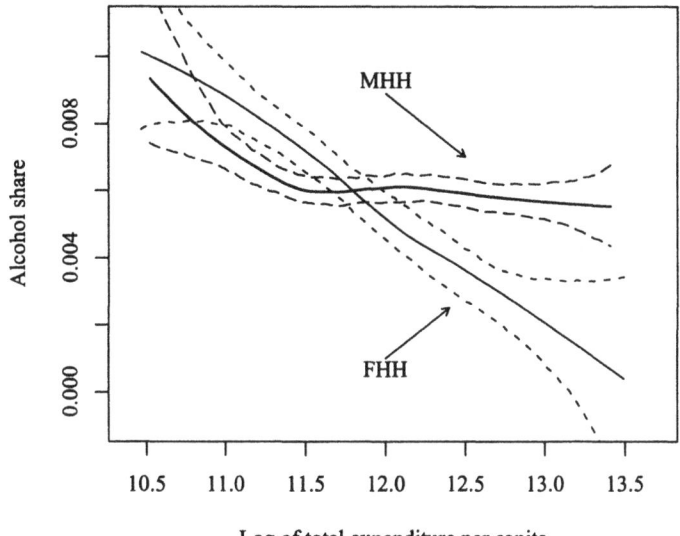

that has been used for calculating the parameters of the index model (see appendix 4.2.). The estimated shift and scales are used to superimpose the curves by transforming the data of FHH. Then, the residual sum of squares of each curve separately is calculated as well as the sum of squares for the pooled data set. The test checks whether the weighted combination of the sum of squares of the individual curves is significantly different from the sum of squares of the pooled data. If the test statistic is significantly different from zero the curves are not parallel. The test statistic $\Upsilon$ follows a standard normal distribution and exhibits values that in all cases, but for education, are large enough to reject the parallelity of the curves at the 5 percent level. These results together with the significant distance between the curves establish that the demand for the different goods appears to follow a different path for FHH and MHH.

The non-parallelity as well as the different expenditure shares suggest that the expenditure elasticities differ between household categories as well, because the expenditure share and the slope of the Engel curve determine the size of the elasticity. Table 18 shows estimates of expenditure elasticities of the different goods categories for each household type. The elasticities are calculated by using the fact that

$$\frac{\partial w_{ijk}(p,x)}{\partial \ln x_{ij}} = w_{ijk}E_x^j - w_{ijk} \qquad (49)$$

**Figure 7: Budget shares for tobacco in FHH and MHH**

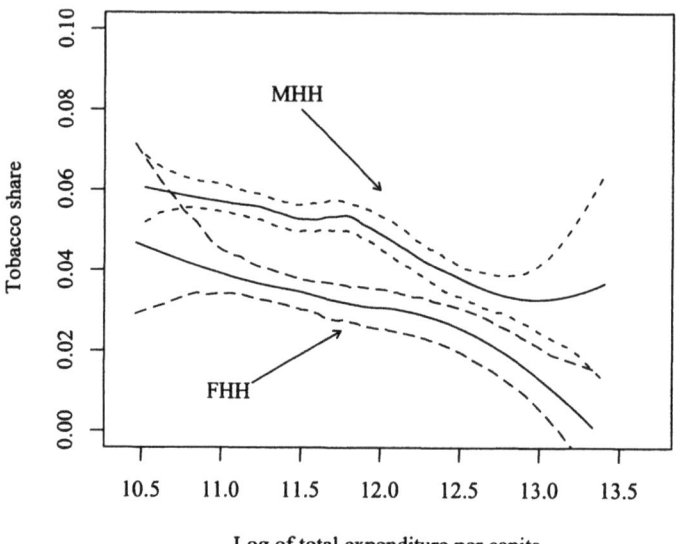

Log of total expenditure per capita

where $E_x^i$ is the expenditure elasticity of the $i$th good with respect to total expenditure $x_{ij}$ and $w_{ijk}$ is the respective budget share. Given an estimate for $\frac{\partial w_{ijk}(p,x)}{\partial \ln x_{ij}}$ the elasticity can be calculated as

$$E_x^j = \frac{(\partial w_{ijk}(p,x)/\partial \ln x_{ij})}{w_{ijk}} + 1 \qquad (50)$$

To obtain the derivative $\frac{\partial w_{ijk}(p,x)}{\partial \ln x_{ij}}$, Ullah (1988) and Rilstone and Ullah (1989) propose the point estimator for the $i$th observation

$$\widehat{\frac{\partial w_{ijk}(p,x)}{\partial \ln x_{ij}}} = \frac{1}{2h}(\hat{m}(x_{ij}+h) - \hat{m}(x_{ij}-h)) \qquad (51)$$

Now substitute in (50) $n^{-1}\sum_n \widehat{\frac{\partial w_{ijk}(p,x)}{\partial \ln x_{ij}}}$ for $\frac{(\partial w_{ijk}(p,x)}{\partial \ln x_{ij})}$ and $n^{-1}\sum_n w_{ijk}$ for $w_{ijk}$ to calculate average elasticities.

The estimated elasticities reported in 19 confirm the pattern given by the demand curves. The table gives the average elasticities as well as expenditure level specific estimates which are calculated for the 20th, 40th, 60th, 80th, and 100th quintiles, which denote the ranges from zero to 20, 20 to 40, etc., quintiles. Differences in responses to changes of expenditure are particularly significant for alcohol and tobacco demand. Among the poorest FHH, tobacco is an inferior good while MHH treat it as a luxury. The elasticities for FHH subsequently fall with rising expenditure to a relatively low level, which holds particularly for alcohol. In contrast, the elasticities of MHH appear to be relatively stable, although they slightly fall for tobacco at the upper end of expenditure. The average elasticity for food is relatively close to 1 among both household categories which is quite large.[38] The food expenditure elasticities for FHH are larger compared to those of MHH. This implies that with increasing expenditure, the food shares in FHH decrease at a slower rate compared to MHH. The elasticities for clothing and education do not differ substantially across the range of total expenditure, although those for education are slightly larger at the lower ranges.

The results presented so far establish different patterns of expenditure among FHH and MHH regarding the different child and adult goods. The results, however, do not allow yet for inference on the welfare of children. Only the curves generated for child clothing allow this conclusion as this is an exclusive child good. Whether children really affect household demand requires the analysis of the parameters of the model.

### 4.4.4 Household expenditure and children

The parametric part of the models is given in tables 21 to 25. To compare the parameters across models, I apply a Chow-like Wald test. Let $\hat{V}$ denote the variance-covariance matrix and $\hat{\beta}$ the estimated parameters generated by the regressions using FHH and MHH data respectively. A Wald test for the equality of the parameters across the two models of the form

$$W = (\hat{\beta}_{fhh} - \hat{\beta}_{mhh})'(\hat{V}_{fhh} + \hat{V}_{mhh})^{-1}(\hat{\beta}_{fhh} - \hat{\beta}_{mhh}) \sim \chi_k^2 \qquad (52)$$

yields the results reported in table 20. All sets of parameters, but those for alcohol, turn out to be significantly different at the 5 percent level for MHH and FHH. For food demand, the coefficients of the log of household size are negative for both types of households, implying that larger households have smaller per capita food expenditures. This finding corresponds to the results of Deaton and Paxson (1998), who demonstrate a negative relationship between household size and expenditure for food for several household surveys from developed and developing countries. This result is contrary to the expectation that because food is an entirely private good there are no economies of scale.

Small children do not affect food demand in neither household category. The same result applies to children in FHH of the age category 5 to 10 years. Older girls impose a negative effect in FHH as well as adult males and females do. Within MHH, boys from age 5 to 10 positively affect food demand while neither juveniles nor adults of any sex appear to influence MHH food demand. The

---
[38] Behrman and Deolalikar (1987) report for India an expenditure elasticity for food that even exceeds one.

results imply that FHH distribute food equally among small children and do not discriminate between sexes. Changes of food demand patterns are mainly governed by adults as well as by total household size. This is even more pronounced for MHH where food demand is almost entirely determined by household size and not by demographic composition, although the positive parameter for boys age 5 to 10 implies discrimination against girls in this age category. However, in this respect the important result is the coefficient for household size which is larger for MHH meaning that an additional household member regardless of which age and sex decrease the food share at a larger rate. This is different among FHH, where the negative parameters for juvenile girls and adults imply that food shares decrease particularly due to these groups. All other effects of additional household members are governed by total household size where the estimate is smaller in absolute value suggesting, that small children fare on average better within FHH. This effect becomes even more pronounced when recalling that food shares among FHH are already higher. These positive results in terms of child welfare in FHH are slightly dampened by the observation that female education decreases food spending in FHH at a faster rate as compared to MHH.

Total household size exerts no effect on child clothing demand within FHH but does so in MHH. The household composition parameters for children are significant in both models and are consistently larger within MHH compared to FHH. Interestingly, both models reveal a slight preference for girls from age zero to 10, which may be explained by possible higher prices for girl's clothing. Adults in FHH affect household demand for child clothing negatively while the respective estimates in MHH are positive though not significant at the 5 percent level. The parameters suggest that demand for child clothing is less responsive to an additional child in FHH. This may not tell the entire story, if women as head of household are more engaged in the maintenance of child clothing. Education exhibits a pattern different from clothing. Household size exerts a larger, positive influence on household expenditure for education in FHH. Estimates for juveniles are positive in both household categories, but larger in FHH. Given the fact that education expenditure is due for children of age 6+, the fact that FHH parameters for small children are negative and larger in absolute value indicates a more efficient allocation of resources spent on education within FHH. As for clothing, both household categories exhibit a slight preference for girls of school age. Another interesting finding is that no differences between rural and urban households are apparent in FHH, while rural MHH spend significantly less on education. Furthermore, the effect from education on clothing expenditure is larger within FHH. In total, the results for child clothing do not reveal larger preferences for children in FHH while the coefficients from the education model suggest that more money is devoted to children in FHH compared to MHH.

Demographic composition estimates reveal a surprising pattern for tobacco and alcohol. All parameters concerning the shares of children are significant and positive. This is a surprising result as it seems to suggest that children participate in the consumption of alcohol and tobacco. It is difficult to explain such pattern and only a few ad hoc explanations are available: (i) the excluded category 'elder people beyond age 60' significantly decrease consumption of tobacco and alcohol, (ii) cigarettes and alcohol consumption is related to greater fertility, (iii) cigarette and alcohol consumption works as a compensation for stress that is exerted from children. Regarding the first explanation, all demographic share parameters need to be interpreted with respect to the excluded category elderly people[39]. Dropping small children and including the share of elderly in the equations turns the signs of almost all parameters into negative, while many lose their significance. The parameter for the share of elderly people above age 60 is negative and significant. Testing the reasoning behind the other two arguments, which are highly speculative, is beyond the scope of this paper and cannot be done given the data.

In interpreting the parameters for alcohol and tobacco it is revealing to consider again the fact that among FHH only 16 percent purchase any tobacco and 20 percent spend money on alcohol. The shares of MHH purchasing tobacco and alcohol are larger and amount to 30 and 31 percent respectively. Given such different expenditure propensities, the first stage probit models are useful for investigating the decision of purchasing these goods at all.

Table 26 shows the marginal effects of the first stage probit estimations for education and child clothing. The marginal effects for children of the clothing model are slightly larger among MHH, although the difference between household categories is not substantial. However, this difference is compensated by the fact that FHH generally spend more on clothing compared with MHH. The same holds for education where the coefficients representing children imply that MHH are more responsive to children when investing in education. Again, FHH generally spend slightly more on education although this difference is not significant.

The demographic coefficients for alcohol and tobacco reveal a very clear pattern: children in FHH reduce expenditure on adult goods, while the respective coefficients for MHH are even positive for alcohol. Child share estimates are negative and significant for tobacco, but are in size always more than twice the value of MHH coefficients. A further interesting result is that among FHH, male adults appear to be the driving force behind the decision to consume tobacco which becomes apparent from the significantly positive coefficient, while the respective parameter in MHH is insignificant. Adult females on the other hand, negatively affect the purchasing decision in both categories, although the absolute effect is larger in MHH.

---

[39]This is similar with dummy variables indicating a set of qualitative characteristics, where one dummy has to be excluded to avoid multicollinearity. All resulting dummy coefficients need to be evaluated against the excluded category.

## 4.4 The old-age security hypothesis

The old-age security hypothesis predicts that in the absence of savings, parents invest more in health and education of their children. One basic means to secure health is adequate nourishment, which can be achieved through a diet that provides not only calories but also necessary vitamins. The latter is often contained in food which is more expensive as for example vegetables and fruits. Education often implies an improvement of productivity and an increased likelihood to find a job on the wage labor market. Higher incomes lead to a larger set of options to financially support parents during old age. Therefore, educating children may be regarded as a means to secure old age security through remittances.

The variable used to indicate alternatives to children as old age security is savings. Unfortunately, the available data contains no information on the amount of the savings account, but only indicate if the household saves. The other means to secure old age welfare are assets. These assets are difficult to capture as not many are useful as an old age security investment due to their depreciation over time. The most effective asset is probably land, but given the underdeveloped markets for land and the precarious situation of land rights of women in Tanzania (Yngstrom 2002), it can hardly be regarded as an old age security for women. Including the size of available land in the regressions does not yield any significant results–neither for FHH nor MHH. Consequently, in what follows I rely on savings only.

In the first step, I introduce the savings dummy into the demand equations for food and education. Secondly, I add 6 interaction terms, where the share of each child age and sex group in total household size is interacted with the savings variable to investigate how the presence of children in the demand equations responds to savings. If FHH invest in children because of the lack of options to save money for old age, then the savings variable should yield a negative parameter. The savings parameter in the food demand equations reported in table 28 turns out to be significantly negative in both, FHH and MHH, regressions. The absolute value of the parameter is larger in FHH than in MHH; households that save spend on average between 6 and 4 percentage points less for food, respectively. To compare the impact from savings on food demand in the two household categories, I impose the savings effect on the demand curve which is graphed in figure 8. The dashed line denotes the curves from MHH, while the confidence intervals are left out to facilitate the exposition. The graph reveals that after imposing the impact from savings, the demand curves coincide fairly well compared to the benchmarks for 'non-savers' located above the curve denoting the 'savers'. This result is conform to the hypothesis that parents invest in children to secure support in times of old age. The graph further shows that demand patterns become much more similar for FHH and MHH, when both have the option to save money.

The interaction terms capture the impact of savings on the demographic parameters. None of the interaction terms is significant at the 5 percent level in FHH. Children therefore do not appear to have much influence on the negative impact of savings on food demand. In MHH, almost all interactions are insignificant as well. The coefficient for the interaction between juvenile boys and savings is significantly negative in MHH, implying that this group even increases the effect from savings on food demand. Judging from the results of the food regressions, one may conclude that children are an investment good in both household categories. The higher food demand among FHH disappears as soon as a control for savings is introduced.

Regarding education, savings increase the budget share of education for both household categories. This may suggest that household heads save for the education of their children at older ages. But the interaction terms are all, but for girls of age 11 to 15, negative and significant for MHH implying that the positive impact of savings on education spending decreases with more children. Within FHH, only boys of age 5 to 10 and juvenile girls significantly reduce the positive impact of saving on educational spending. Even though, savings increase expenditure on education, the positive effect diminishes with increasing shares of children living in the household. The graph with savings imposed on the demand curves (figure 9) reveals that differences between MHH and FHH even become more pronounced among savers and non-savers.

In sum, the results from the education regressions do neither support nor reject the old age hypothesis since the positive effect running from savings on education implies a rejection while the negative interaction terms qualify the positive effect and rather speak for support the old age security assumption. It is unfortunately not obvious from the results whether households save for the education of their children or for the participation in adult training programs. Furthermore, it is not possible to conclude that households save for education at all and whether the savings variable captures another effect running from saving on education. Nevertheless, the results reveal some interesting patterns. It appears that among savers, spending on food and education is rather a substitute than a complement.

The test is subject to a number of problems: (i) the overall spread of saving accounts is rather low and therefore, savings may not represent all options that households have to accumulate assets. This might be particularly true for rural areas, where formal savings institutions are rarely available. However, the rural-urban dummy variable accounts to some extent for this fact. The major asset for rural households is land, which is almost a non-tradable good, since land is largely allocated through family relations (Yngstrom 2002) which might explain the insignificant coefficients for land. (ii) The results are difficult to interpret as savings are meant for future consumption while the measured expenditure shares refer to current consumption. (iii) Health and education may not be regarded by parents as a means to achieve improved old age support. (iv) The relationship between savings and spending might be dependent on the level of income. In the present

**Figure 8: Food demand curves for savers and non-savers**

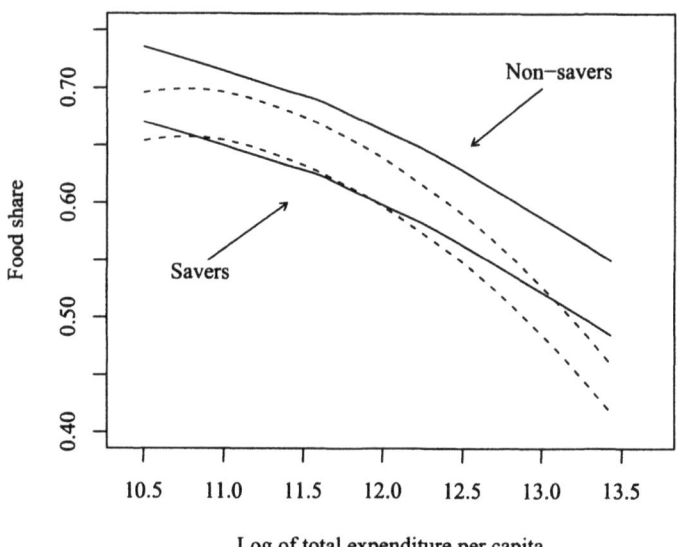

Log of total expenditure per capita

formulation, the savings parameter is assumed to be stable across the whole range of expenditure. However, it is likely that poorer households do not have sufficient monetary surplus that would allow them to save enough to keep their living standard during old age. But these are the households where it is expected that households need child support and ergo healthy and well educated children most. (v) Increased expenditure for food may not be associated with improved nourishment and health. The data does unfortunately not allow for deriving the nutritional status of children within saving households in order to trace different compositions of the food baskets among savers and non-savers. However, it has been found for Malawi that children from FHH exhibits higher levels of nourishment (Kennedy and Peters 1992). Although the authors do not report spending behavior of the households, the finding fits to the higher food share found in Tanzania.

## 4.4 Conclusions

In this study I have investigated patterns of demand and their implications for child welfare across FHH and MHH. The results reveal significantly different expenditure patterns where FHH spend more toward the welfare of their children and less on personal consumption of the adult goods alcohol and tobacco. The findings on the old age hypothesis demonstrate despite their weaknesses a significant rela-

**Figure 9: Education demand curves for savers and non-savers**

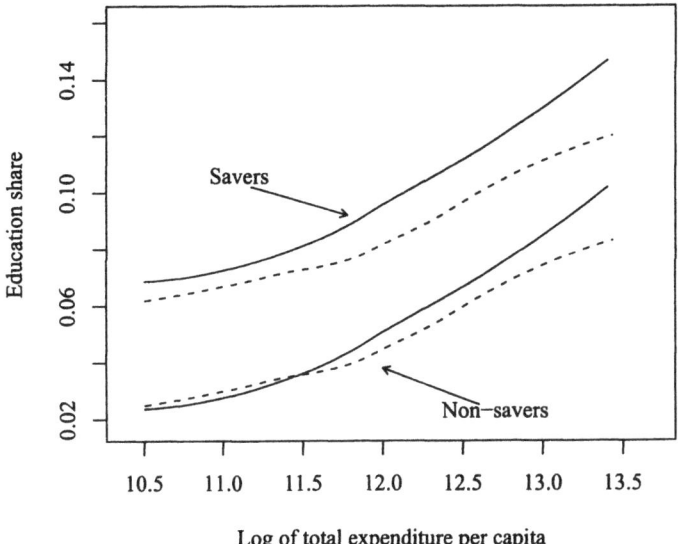

tionship between savings and spending. Savings significantly reduce spending for food in both household categories. The demand patterns become even very similar after imposing the influence of savings on the demand curves. This finding is consistent with the old age security hypothesis. According to this, FHH spend more on food because the women treat children as an investment good. This explanation is in contrast to the common view that women spend more on children because they are and get closer to them during pregnancy, birth and subsequent child hood. However, the results from the education regressions do not unambiguously support the old age hypothesis since education spending increases with savings. Although the presence of children overcompensates the positive effect it is not easy to think of explanations for this finding. One possibility is, that parents save and spend rather on their own education and adult training programs as on the education of their children. Unfortunately, the data does not differentiate between spending on child or adult education. If this is true, then this finding would further support the old age hypothesis. However, further research is needed in order to differentiate between spending on adult and child training and that allows for including the amount of savings available in order to track dependencies of the link between savings and spending behavior across different levels of income. The results should therefore be treated as a first step in the testing of the old age security hypothesis.

The treatment of FHH as a single category is likely to be oversimplistic and may hide parts of the true relationship, particularly with regard to old age security. In the analysis, it was assumed that regarding consumption, FHH act free of restrictions like male control over the household budget which may not be the truth for all possible categories (see also the discussion and results on disaggregation of FHH in chapter 2). Widowed women with children at school age are probably more prone to treat their children as investment goods. This effect becomes stronger with lower prospects of remarriage as the woman is in many societies socially restricted to get further children without being married. The same may hold true for divorced women. However, in households comprising three generations, the grandmother may treated as a the head of household, although she may not the one actually doing the decisions. Differentiating between these groups might change the results. Further research on this topic is needed in order to differentiate more sharply between FHH categories on the basis of the true household decision maker. Unfortunately, data on such disaggregation other than marital status and demographic characteristics is not available in the current data set.

The findings are also relevant for the literature on intrahousehold bargaining over resources. On the one hand, the results support the common finding that women spend more on the welfare of their children. Policies that transfer money to mothers and not to fathers are more likely to translate into increases of child welfare as if the money would be given to fathers. This assumption has been fruitfully applied in the Mexican PROGRESA project, where child education has significantly improved. If the motive behind the higher spending of women is grounded in the old security motive, then policies that grant monetary transfers to mothers exclusively may fail under circumstances where women have other means to insure against old age poverty. More research on this subject would be useful, particularly in the context of developing and developed countries, where in the latter, the conditions for old age security which is independent from children are more likely to hold. Studies on spending behavior and welfare of children are mostly restricted to the developing world. To arrive at a conclusion on this matter, however, such comparisons are needed.

The results unfortunately do not allow whether the higher spending affects child nutrition and particularly their health status. Biophysical data on this subject would be needed to obtain further insights into this issue. Such data is unfortunately difficult to get, since measurement even of simple indicators like the body mass index substantially increases the effort of data collection. Calculating caloric consumption from simple expenditure data is not sufficient as it does not allow to obtain insights on nutritious content of the food. This is particularly so, if the choice of food quality differs systematically across household types. Food that is more expensive on the other hand may not necessarily imply that it is of higher quality.

# A Appendix 4.1

## Table 16: Summary statistics

|  | FHH | | MHH | |
| --- | --- | --- | --- | --- |
|  | Mean | Standard dev. | Mean | Standard dev. |
| Food share | 0.666 | 0.145 | 0.637 | 0.152 |
| Alcohol share | 0.014 | 0.056 | 0.024 | 0.066 |
| Tobacco share | 0.032 | 0.045 | 0.049 | 0.063 |
| Education share | 0.047 | 0.071 | 0.044 | 0.068 |
| Clothing share | 0.028 | 0.031 | 0.025 | 0.031 |
| Log Expenditure per capita | 11.864 | 0.652 | 11.884 | 0.631 |
| Log Hhldsize | 1.159 | 0.660 | 1.415 | 0.656 |
| Boys 0-4 | 0.064 | 0.132 | 0.072 | 0.119 |
| Girls 0-4 | 0.064 | 0.132 | 0.072 | 0.118 |
| Boys 5-10 | 0.062 | 0.123 | 0.063 | 0.107 |
| Girls 5-10 | 0.068 | 0.129 | 0.060 | 0.105 |
| Boys 11-15 | 0.052 | 0.112 | 0.043 | 0.089 |
| Girls 11-15 | 0.058 | 0.120 | 0.043 | 0.088 |
| Male adults | 0.102 | 0.161 | 0.337 | 0.258 |
| Female adults | 0.423 | 0.290 | 0.247 | 0.155 |
| Primary education | 0.387 | 0.487 | 0.526 | 0.499 |
| Secondary education | 0.093 | 0.291 | 0.161 | 0.368 |
| Age | 44.028 | 15.291 | 42.524 | 14.295 |
| Rural | 0.312 | 0.463 | 0.363 | 0.481 |
| Log available land | 0.755 | 0.783 | 0.964 | 0.939 |
| Savings | 0.091 | 0.288 | 0.142 | 0.349 |

## Table 17: Shares of households purchasing goods

|  | Purchase FHH | | Purchase MHH | |
| --- | --- | --- | --- | --- |
|  | Yes | No | Yes | No |
| Alcohol | 0.20 | 0.80 | 0.30 | 0.70 |
| Tobacco | 0.16 | 0.84 | 0.31 | 0.69 |
| Clothing | 0.60 | 0.40 | 0.65 | 0.35 |
| Education | 0.51 | 0.49 | 0.52 | 0.48 |

## Table 18: Estimated scale and shift parameters*

|  | Food | Clothing | Education | Alcohol | Tobacco |
|---|---|---|---|---|---|
| Scale Parameter $\alpha$ | 0.037 | 0.002 | 0.006 | −0.001 | −0.016 |
|  | (0.002) | (0.001) | (0.001) | (0.000) | (0.002) |
| Shift Parameter $\delta$ | 0.170 | −0.110 | 0.110 | 0.040 | −0.160 |
|  | (0.037) | (0.143) | (0.082) | (0.251) | (0.431) |
| $\Upsilon$ | 13.043 | 1.450 | 1.310 | 8.075 | 11.997 |
| p | 0.000 | 0.147 | 0.190 | 0.000 | 0.000 |

*Associated p-values in parentheses.

## Table 19: Estimated expenditure elasticities

|  | Food | | Clothing | | Education | | Tobacco | | Alcohol | |
|---|---|---|---|---|---|---|---|---|---|---|
|  | FHH | MHH | FHH | MHH | FHH | MHH | FHH | MHH | FHH | MHH |
| $E_j^x$ | 0.94 | 0.91 | 1.16 | 1.01 | 1.40 | 1.38 | 0.77 | 0.93 | 0.53 | 0.90 |
| 20 | 0.97 | 0.96 | 1.12 | 1.13 | 1.18 | 1.15 | 0.85 | 1.01 | 0.81 | 0.95 |
| 40 | 0.94 | 0.93 | 1.11 | 1.18 | 1.39 | 1.30 | 0.81 | 0.98 | 0.56 | 0.78 |
| 60 | 0.93 | 0.91 | 1.13 | 1.16 | 1.48 | 1.44 | 0.80 | 0.94 | 0.38 | 0.97 |
| 80 | 0.93 | 0.89 | 1.17 | 1.15 | 1.46 | 1.47 | 0.83 | 0.85 | 0.46 | 0.95 |
| 100 | 0.91 | 0.85 | 1.23 | 1.17 | 1.40 | 1.41 | 0.45 | 0.86 | 0.25 | 0.95 |

## Table 20: Wald test for difference of parameters

|  | Food | Clothing | Clothing | Alcohol | Tobacco |
|---|---|---|---|---|---|
| $\chi_{32}^2$ | 75.809 | 50.441 | 48.603 | 73.694 | 33.900 |
| p-value | 0.000 | 0.020 | 0.030 | 0.000 | 0.376 |

Patterns of Demand

## Table 21: Parameters of the semiparametric model - Food

| | FHH | | MHH | |
|---|---|---|---|---|
| | Parameter | t-value | Parameter | t-value |
| ln Hhldsize | −0.048 ** | −12.656 | −0.063 ** | −24.197 |
| Boys 0-4 | −0.001 | −0.104 | 0.013 | 1.320 |
| Girls 0-4 | 0.006 | 0.405 | −0.000 | −0.037 |
| Boys 5-10 | 0.001 | 0.046 | 0.045 ** | 4.006 |
| Girls 5-10 | −0.006 | −0.436 | 0.018 | 1.593 |
| Boys 11-15 | −0.027 | −1.642 | −0.005 | −0.393 |
| Girls 11-15 | −0.031 ** | −2.039 | −0.020 | −1.511 |
| Male adults | −0.027 ** | −2.189 | −0.005 | −0.841 |
| Female adults | −0.039 ** | −4.516 | −0.012 ** | −1.484 |
| Primary education | −0.029 ** | −5.807 | −0.019 ** | −6.456 |
| Secondary education | −0.086 ** | −11.292 | −0.051 ** | −13.411 |
| Age | −0.000 | −0.094 | 0.000 ** | 4.713 |
| Rural | 0.029 ** | 6.722 | 0.029 ** | 11.754 |
| F | 20.346 | $p : 0.000$ | 59.491 | $p : 0.000$ |
| N | 4,737 | | 14,046 | |

** significant at 5 percent level

## Table 22: Parameters of the semiparametric model - Clothing

|  | FHH Parameter | t-value | MHH Parameter | t-value |
|---|---|---|---|---|
| ln Hhldsize | 0.002 | 1.028 | 0.002 ** | 2.340 |
| Boys 0-4 | 0.032 ** | 8.522 | 0.043 ** | 13.781 |
| Girls 0-4 | 0.036 ** | 9.510 | 0.046 ** | 14.718 |
| Boys 5-10 | 0.029 ** | 7.272 | 0.039 ** | 12.468 |
| Girls 5-10 | 0.032 ** | 8.291 | 0.046 ** | 14.522 |
| Boys 11-15 | 0.019 ** | 4.585 | 0.038 ** | 11.267 |
| Girls 11-15 | 0.031 ** | 7.283 | 0.037 ** | 10.459 |
| Male adults | −0.019 ** | −3.538 | 0.001 | 0.197 |
| Female adults | −0.006 | −1.424 | 0.004 | 1.092 |
| Primary education | 0.004 ** | 2.657 | 0.003 ** | 3.257 |
| Secondary education | 0.007 ** | 3.295 | 0.004 ** | 3.805 |
| Age | 0.000 | 0.017 | 0.000 ** | −3.179 |
| Rural | −0.004 ** | −3.372 | −0.005 ** | −7.531 |
| Mills | 0.015 ** | 5.013 | 0.012 ** | 5.955 |
| F | 5.218 | p : 0.000 | 14.230 | p : 0.000 |
| N | 3,067 |  | 9,903 |  |

** significant at 5-percent level

## Table 23: Parameters of the semiparametric model - Education

|  | FHH Parameter | t-value | MHH Parameter | t-value |
|---|---|---|---|---|
| ln Hhldsize | 0.058 ** | 8.748 | 0.050 ** | 14.483 |
| Boys 0-4 | −0.027 | −1.815 | −0.026 ** | −2.764 |
| Girls 0-4 | −0.034 ** | −2.191 | −0.024 ** | −2.529 |
| Boys 5-10 | 0.061 ** | 5.939 | 0.058 ** | 7.878 |
| Girls 5-10 | 0.104 ** | 10.075 | 0.071 ** | 9.380 |
| Boys 11-15 | 0.152 ** | 11.563 | 0.131 ** | 15.349 |
| Girls 11-15 | 0.144 ** | 11.527 | 0.139 ** | 15.987 |
| Male adults | 0.057 ** | 5.329 | 0.080 ** | 13.888 |
| Female adults | 0.066 ** | 7.561 | 0.053 ** | 7.116 |
| Primary education | 0.015 ** | 4.164 | 0.017 ** | 8.734 |
| Secondary education | 0.041 ** | 7.826 | 0.041 ** | 17.536 |
| Age | 0.001 ** | 4.846 | 0.001 ** | 12.315 |
| Rural | −0.005 | −1.746 | −0.009 ** | −5.388 |
| Mills | 0.065 ** | 6.724 | 0.049 ** | 10.500 |
| F | 10.119 | p : 0.000 | 37.803 | p : 0.000 |
| N | 2,571 |  | 7,934 |  |

** significant at 5 percent level

## Table 24: Parameters of the semiparametric model - Tobacco

|                    | FHH        |         | MHH        |         |
|                    | Parameter  | t-value | Parameter  | t-value |
|--------------------|------------|---------|------------|---------|
| ln Hhldsize        | −0.018 **  | −5.616  | −0.034 **  | −16.786 |
| Boys 0-4           | 0.036 **   | 2.604   | 0.063 **   | 8.598   |
| Girls 0-4          | 0.041 **   | 3.162   | 0.054 **   | 7.020   |
| Boys 5-10          | 0.038 **   | 3.006   | 0.069 **   | 6.903   |
| Girls 5-10         | 0.044 **   | 3.305   | 0.056 **   | 5.866   |
| Boys 11-15         | 0.051 **   | 3.837   | 0.045 **   | 4.947   |
| Girls 11-15        | 0.030 **   | 2.141   | 0.074 **   | 6.433   |
| Male adults        | 0.028 **   | 2.148   | 0.026 **   | 5.168   |
| Female adults      | 0.025 **   | 3.454   | 0.038 **   | 4.660   |
| Primary education  | 0.004      | 0.745   | 0.017 **   | 3.965   |
| Secondary education| 0.001      | 0.068   | 0.030 **   | 3.017   |
| Age                | 0.000      | −0.039  | 0.000      | −1.181  |
| Rural              | −0.015 **  | −3.560  | −0.029 **  | −5.740  |
| Mills              | −0.037 **  | −2.893  | −0.089 **  | −3.774  |
| F                  | 1.779      | p : 0.005 | 16.769   | p : 0.000 |
| N                  | 848        |         | 4,798      |         |

** significant at 5 percent level

## Table 25: Parameters of the semiparametric model - Alcohol

|                    | FHH        |         | MHH        |         |
|                    | Parameter  | t-value | Parameter  | t-value |
|--------------------|------------|---------|------------|---------|
| ln Hhldsize        | −0.006 **  | −4.984  | −0.004 **  | −8.816  |
| Boys 0-4           | 0.003      | 1.307   | 0.004 **   | 4.148   |
| Girls 0-4          | 0.003      | 1.049   | 0.003 **   | 2.961   |
| Boys 5-10          | 0.006 **   | 2.622   | 0.006 **   | 5.263   |
| Girls 5-10         | 0.009 **   | 2.846   | 0.004 **   | 3.071   |
| Boys 11-15         | 0.009 **   | 2.756   | 0.005 **   | 3.487   |
| Girls 11-15        | 0.005 **   | 2.072   | 0.006 **   | 4.137   |
| Male adults        | 0.004 **   | 2.396   | 0.006 **   | 7.215   |
| Female adults      | 0.006 **   | 4.206   | 0.002 **   | 2.259   |
| Primary education  | 0.001      | −0.321  | 0.000      | −1.043  |
| Secondary education| 0.000      | −0.676  | 0.001      | 1.759   |
| Age                | 0.000      | −0.603  | 0.000 **   | 4.702   |
| Rural              | −0.003     | −1.418  | 0.003 **   | 2.919   |
| Mills              | −0.012 **  | −2.188  | 0.008 **   | 2.698   |
| F                  | 2.869      | p : 0.000 | 16.503   | p : 0.000 |
| N                  | 995        |         | 4466       |         |

** significant at 5 percent level

Table 26: First stage probit models - Clothing and education

| | Clothing | | | | Education | | | |
|---|---|---|---|---|---|---|---|---|
| | FHH | | MHH | | FHH | | MHH | |
| | Parameter | t-value | Parameter | t-value | Parameter | t-value | Parameter | t-value |
| Ln Expend. per cap. | 0.886** | 2.430 | 0.896** | 4.345 | 0.993** | 2.557 | -0.005** | 20.303 |
| Ln Expend. per cap. squared | -0.032** | -2.086 | -0.032** | -3.714 | -0.033** | -2.045 | | |
| ln Hhldsize | 0.284** | 14.342 | 0.194** | 18.038 | 0.454** | 20.732 | 0.455** | 32.390 |
| Boys 0-4 | 1.239** | 14.044 | 1.435** | 26.336 | -0.157 | -1.666 | -0.165** | -2.652 |
| Girls 0-4 | 1.294** | 14.264 | 1.378** | 25.254 | -0.241** | -2.525 | -0.176** | -2.813 |
| Boys 5-10 | 1.064** | 11.990 | 1.008** | 18.811 | 0.719** | 7.689 | 0.914** | 14.251 |
| Girls 5-10 | 0.959** | 11.475 | 1.004** | 18.273 | 0.875** | 9.670 | 1.059** | 16.096 |
| Boys 11-15 | 0.796** | 9.067 | 0.850** | 15.015 | 1.462** | 14.070 | 1.631** | 20.953 |
| Girls 11-15 | 0.681** | 8.265 | 0.686** | 11.895 | 1.354** | 13.808 | 1.630** | 20.372 |
| Male adults | -0.026 | -0.360 | 0.028 | 0.848 | 0.145 | 1.786 | 0.315** | 7.253 |
| Female adults | 0.037 | 0.717 | 0.133** | 3.380 | 0.190** | 3.135 | -0.023 | -0.467 |
| Primary education | 0.020 | 0.946 | -0.003 | -0.299 | 0.092** | 4.123 | 0.103** | 7.919 |
| Secondary education | -0.032 | -0.992 | -0.016 | -1.114 | 0.183** | 5.394 | 0.186** | 11.159 |
| Age | -0.003** | -3.725 | -0.002** | -5.227 | 0.001 | 1.572 | 0.004** | 6.900 |
| Rural | -0.009 | -0.498 | 0.010 | 1.117 | -0.001** | -3.495 | -0.032** | -2.905 |
| Constant | -18.401** | -3.040 | -21.782** | -5.319 | -20.296** | -3.491 | -9.169** | -26.064 |
| Pseudo R-square | 0.382 | | 0.403 | | 0.3547 | | 0.3782 | |
| LR Test $\chi^2_{(33)}$ | 2483.34 | p : 0.000 | 7205.17 | p : 0.000 | 2423.45 | p : 0.000 | 7607.86 | p : 0.000 |
| LR Test $\chi^2_{(1)}$ | 4.350 | p : 0.037 | 13.74 | p : 0.000 | 4.19 | p : 0.041 | 0.69 | p : 0.406 |
| N | 4,737 | | 14,046 | | 4,737 | | 14,046 | |

** significant at 5 percent level

Table 27: First stage probit models - Alcohol and tobacco

| | Alcohol | | | | Tobacco | | | |
|---|---|---|---|---|---|---|---|---|
| | FHH | | MHH | | FHH | | MHH | |
| | Parameter | t-value | Parameter | t-value | Parameter | t-value | Parameter | t-value |
| Ln Expend. per cap. | −0.752** | −2.944 | −0.288 | −1.422 | 0.002 | 0.190 | 0.009 | 1.152 |
| Ln Expend. per cap. squared | 0.034** | 3.214 | 0.016 | 1.895 | 0.085** | 7.303 | 0.036** | 3.443 |
| ln Hhldsize | 0.072** | 5.330 | 0.037** | 3.464 | −0.231** | −4.409 | −0.063 | −1.279 |
| Boys 0-4 | −0.103 | −1.733 | 0.167** | 3.402 | −0.253** | −4.752 | −0.065 | −1.302 |
| Girls 0-4 | −0.086 | −1.447 | 0.101** | 2.016 | −0.276** | −5.186 | −0.178** | −3.520 |
| Boys 5-10 | −0.087 | −1.448 | 0.155** | 3.066 | −0.251** | −4.905 | −0.144** | −2.804 |
| Girls 5-10 | −0.183** | −3.098 | 0.043 | 0.825 | −0.257** | −4.761 | −0.092 | −1.640 |
| Boys 11-15 | −0.185** | −2.934 | 0.085 | 1.502 | −0.272** | −5.148 | −0.226** | −3.883 |
| Girls 11-15 | −0.144** | −2.384 | 0.093 | 1.606 | 0.086** | 2.139 | 0.030 | 0.972 |
| Male adults | 0.075 | 1.519 | 0.161** | 5.109 | −0.120** | −4.459 | −0.158** | −4.153 |
| Female adults | −0.035 | −1.042 | 0.040 | 1.038 | −0.063** | −4.963 | −0.079** | −7.788 |
| Primary education | −0.024 | −1.626 | −0.033** | −3.142 | −0.112** | −6.390 | −0.172** | −13.313 |
| Secondary education | −0.034 | −1.555 | 0.000 | −0.008 | 0.001 | 1.136 | 0.001** | 2.626 |
| Age | −0.001 | −1.834 | 0.002** | 5.096 | 0.073** | 6.387 | 0.109** | 12.474 |
| Rural | 0.133** | 9.986 | 0.184** | 20.650 | −1.255** | −2.214 | −1.006** | −3.508 |
| Constant | 13.990** | 2.426 | 1.749 | 0.502 | | | | |
| Pseudo R-square | 0.0946 | | 0.0976 | | 0.1281 | | 0.068 | |
| LR Test $\chi^2_{33}$ | 475.45 | p : 0.000 | 1791.4 | p : 0.000 | 573.93 | p : 0.000 | 1267.83 | p : 0.000 |
| LR Test $\chi^2_1$ | 10.23 | p : 0.001 | 3.58 | p : 0.058 | 0.03 | p : 8.874 | 2.11 | p : 0.147 |
| N | 4,737 | | 14,046 | | 4,737 | | 14,046 | |

** significant at 5 percent level

Table 28: Parameters of the old age model - food and education

| | Food | | | | Education | | | |
|---|---|---|---|---|---|---|---|---|
| | FHH Parameter | t-value | MHH Parameter | t-value | FHH Parameter | t-value | MHH Parameter | t-value |
| ln Hhldsize | -0.044** | -10.576 | -0.057** | -20.689 | 0.063** | 6.198 | 0.050** | 11.519 |
| Boys 0-4 | -0.002 | -0.171 | 0.001 | 0.104 | -0.036** | -2.329 | -0.033** | -3.280 |
| Girls 0-4 | 0.000 | 0.002 | -0.008 | -0.799 | -0.043** | -2.269 | -0.030** | -2.915 |
| Boys 5-10 | 0.004 | 0.242 | 0.042 | 3.569 | 0.073** | 7.895 | 0.058** | 8.163 |
| Girls 5-10 | 0.000 | 0.014 | 0.005 | 0.423 | 0.102** | 8.069 | 0.069** | 9.630 |
| Boys 11-15 | -0.030 | -1.821 | 0.000 | 0.020 | 0.165** | 8.196 | 0.130** | 13.051 |
| Girls 11-15 | -0.037** | -2.414 | -0.021 | -1.460 | 0.158** | 9.686 | 0.136** | 12.512 |
| Male adults | -0.021 | -1.666 | -0.011 | -1.615 | 0.048** | 4.166 | 0.064** | 7.970 |
| Female adults | -0.036** | -4.116 | -0.020** | -2.354 | 0.057** | 5.519 | 0.040** | 3.988 |
| Primary education | -0.027** | -5.328 | -0.017** | -5.500 | 0.015** | 4.169 | 0.015** | 8.193 |
| Secondary education | -0.070** | -8.476 | -0.038** | -9.778 | 0.035** | 5.782 | 0.035** | 12.216 |
| Age | 0.000 | 0.110 | 0.000 | 4.414 | 0.001** | 4.282 | 0.001** | 9.325 |
| Rural | 0.028** | 6.192 | 0.027** | 10.487 | -0.006** | -2.069 | -0.009** | -5.722 |
| Savings | -0.065** | -5.004 | -0.042** | -6.347 | 0.045** | 3.793 | 0.037** | 5.915 |
| Boys 0-4 * savings | 0.056 | 1.059 | 0.024 | 0.815 | -0.054 | -1.499 | -0.058** | -2.826 |
| Girls 0-4 * savings | 0.088 | 1.893 | -0.038 | -1.326 | -0.055 | -1.618 | -0.059** | -2.936 |
| Boys 5-10 * savings | 0.037 | 0.679 | -0.035 | -1.205 | -0.118** | -4.088 | -0.074** | -4.182 |
| Girls 5-10 * savings | -0.028 | -0.521 | 0.012 | 0.402 | -0.050 | -1.499 | -0.061** | -3.196 |
| Boys 11-15 * savings | 0.029 | 0.442 | -0.075 | -2.274 | -0.064 | -1.099 | -0.052** | -2.385 |
| Girls 11-15 * savings | 0.086 | 1.596 | -0.020 | -0.572 | -0.083** | -2.461 | -0.037 | -1.585 |
| Mills | | | | | 0.074** | 5.284 | 0.052** | 8.631 |
| F | 20.343 | p : 0.000 | 63.335 | p : 0.000 | 20.343 | p : 0.000 | 63.335 | p : 0.000 |
| N | 4,723 | | 13,981 | | 4,723 | | 13,981 | |

** significant at 5 percent level

# B   Appendix 4.2

## B.1. Estimating the transformation parameters $\alpha$ and $\beta$

The model is estimated by applying the differencing procedure as proposed by Yatchew, Sun and Deri (2003)[40]

$$w_i = m(\ln x_i - \delta z_i) + \alpha z_i + \varepsilon_i \tag{53}$$

The idea is to remove the nonparametric function by differencing it out which has the advantage that in the process of finding the parameter $\alpha$ *and* $\delta$ one does not need to compute the nonparametric function $m(\cdot)$. To achieve this, evaluate the nonparametric function $m(\ln x_i - \delta c_i)$ at some reasonably chosen parameter values $\delta$ and obtain observations $m$. The obervations $(y_1, m_1, z_1), \ldots, (y_n, m_n, z_n)$ have to be arranged with respect to $m_i$ in increasing order such that $m_1 \leq m_2 \leq \cdots \leq m_n$. Next, consider the differencing coefficients $d$ for which the conditions

$$\sum_{i=1}^{J} d_i = 0 \quad \text{and} \quad \sum_{i=1}^{J} d_i^2 = 1 \tag{54}$$

must hold. $J$ denotes here the order of differencing. The differencing coefficients have to arranged in a band matrix

$$D = \begin{pmatrix} d_0, & d_1, & \ldots, & d_j, & 0, & \ldots & 0 \\ 0 & d_0, & d_1, & \ldots, & d_j, & \ldots & 0 \\ \vdots & \vdots & \vdots & \vdots & & & \\ 0, & \ldots & d_0, & d_1, & \ldots & d_j, & 0 \\ 0, & \ldots & 0 & d_0, & d_1, & \ldots & d_j \end{pmatrix} \tag{55}$$

where $D$ is a $(n-j) \times n$ matrix. Next premultiply equation 53 with $D$ and obtain

$$Dy \cong Dm(\ln x - \delta z) + D\alpha z + D\varepsilon \tag{56}$$

Now since $m(\cdot)$ is assumed to be smooth function, the differencing removes the nonparametric effect as the $x_i$ come close. Hence, after removal of $m(\cdot)$, one is left with the equation

$$Dy \cong D\alpha z + Du \tag{57}$$

which can be conviniently estimated by applying OLS. Yatchew (1997) shows that differencing in the context of partial linear models yields parameters which are

$$\hat{\theta} \overset{a}{\sim} \left( \theta, \left(1 + \frac{1}{2j}\right) \frac{\sigma_\varepsilon^2}{NV_u} \right) \tag{58}$$

---

[40]See also Yatchew (1997) and P. Hall and Titterington (1990)

where $\sigma_\epsilon^2$ denotes the variance of the error term of model 57. The estimated parameters follow a normal distribution with

$$n^{1/2}(\hat{\boldsymbol{\theta}} - \boldsymbol{\theta}_0) \overset{a}{\sim} N(\mathbf{0}, \boldsymbol{V}) \qquad (59)$$

### B.2. Testing equality of the regression curves

The test statistic for testing equality of regression curves is calculated as

$$\Upsilon = (mn)^{1/2}(s_p^2 - s_w^2)/[s_w^2(2\hat{\pi})^{1/2}] \sim N(0, 1) \qquad (60)$$

where $s_p^2$ is the differencing estimator of the residual variance of the pooled data, $s_w^2$ is a weighted average of the residual variances of the two regression curves and $\hat{\pi}$ is $\text{tr}(QQ)/NT$, where $Q = P'D'DP - D'D$. $P$ is a permutation matrix that reorders ascendingly the matrix to which it is applied and $D$ is the differencing matrix as defined above. $m$ and $n$ denote the order of differencing the number of observations in the pooled data respectively. See Yatchew (1999) for details.

# 5 Food demand, female headed households, and the estimation of equivalence scales

## 5.5 Introduction

Ever since economists got interested in the analysis of the impact of policies on household welfare they have been searching for a reliable measure thereof. The measurement of welfare is made difficult through the differing demographic composition of households. Obviously, a household with total income $x$ but consisting of a single adult achieves a different level of welfare compared to a family of 2 adults and 3 children which has the same income. The welfare of different households should therefore not be compared using the absolute value of income or alternatively expenditure, but via a measure of welfare that is adjusted to the demographic profile of households. A simple measure is dividing available income or expenditure by the number of household members to arrive at a per capita measure of welfare. However, a difficulty arises from the fact that not all household members consume the same products in the same shares. While there are some goods which can be characterized as public goods like shelter, there are others which are entirely private like food. These private goods are typically consumed in different shares across household members whereas small children usually require less consumption of food as compared to an adult. Another means to achieve welfare comparisons is to employ an equivalence scale, which weights household members according to their actual demand of certain goods. Because of its characteristic of being a private good, food consumption seems to be appropriate to base on the calculation of equivalence scales. This method is referred to as the Engel method, named after Ernst Engel who first suggested to use household budget shares for food as a measure of household welfare. Drawing upon the assumed appropriateness of household food expenditures for measuring welfare, recently a number of approaches have been developed which are based on comparing household food expenditures across different household sizes while applying semiparametric estimation procedures (Pendakur 1999, Yatchew et al. 2003, Stengos, Sun and Wang 2006, Wilke 2004). The goal of these approaches is to estimate the distance between two Engel curves using flexible methods that do not impose any structure on the functional form of the curves.

While some authors have noted that the use of the Engel method is theoretically not well grounded (Nicholson 1976, Pollak and Wales 1979), the plausibility of their arguments still lacks an empirical foundation. This paper aims to fill this gap and to demonstrate the problems associated with determining equivalence scales through comparing household demand for food across female and male headed households in Tanzania. Implicit to the estimation of equivalence scales is the assumption that the only household characteristic that drives the demand for goods is family size and composition. Preferences for certain goods do not play a role in determining demand. This implies that for example in all households all male adults would consume the same (large) portions of food as well as all small girls consume the same (small) portions. But this assumption does not necessarily find support in the empirical literature. A recent body of research addressing household food demand found that food expenditure varies with female bargaining power (Haddad and Hoddinott 1994, Maluccio and Quisumbing 1999) (see also the previous chapter). In order to demonstrate the bias that occurs if characteristics other than household size are correlated with demand, I estimate 'pseudo-equivalence scales' that capture the different preferences for food across female headed households (FHH) and male headed households MHH using the method proposed by Pendakur (1999), Yatchew et al. (2003) and Stengos et al. (2006). In the Engel approach, there should be no difference in food demand related to FHH and MHH.

Sub-Saharan African countries are interesting in this respect as in some countries the incidence of FHH amounts to 30 percent. Furthermore, food constitutes a particularly important consumption good which occupies a large share of total household expenditure. This distinction between household categories appears to be important as the patterns of demand substantially differ between household categories, with FHH spending more on food than MHH. Such behavioral differences bear consequences for the calculation of measures of welfare that are based on food demand. Such measures include the setting of a poverty line or the calculation of adult equivalence scales, the latter being the focus of this paper. The comparison of FHH and MHH is particularly suited for assessing the difference between consumption habits of women and men as it does not rely on any rather crude measure of intrahousehold bargaining power.

The chapter is structured as follows: in section 2, I briefly sketch the difficulties that arise from the estimation of equivalence scales when differences between FHH and MHH are not explicitly taken into account. Section 3 is concerned with FHH in sub-Saharan Africa, and the subsequent section presents the estimation strategy and a discussion of the results.

## 5.5 The estimation of equivalence scales

A number of different theoretical approaches are available to derive equivalence scales and the literature has become numerous (see Van Praag and Warnaar (1993) and Deaton (1997) for extensive reviews and Ebert and Moyes (2003), Ebert (1997), van Praag and Ferrer-i-Carbonell (2004)) and Donaldson and Pendakur (2005) for more recent developments). The methods applied usually aim at computing an index number from the demographic profile of a household that can be used to scale expenditure in order to arrive at a measure of welfare that can be used for comparisons of households of different sizes. Expenditure scaled by this index expresses the amount of money needed to compensate a large family with children to reach the same level of welfare as a reference household which is usually a single adult or a couple without children. It can therefore also be interpreted as a measure of the cost of children. The simplest possible representation of a demographic profile translated into an index is household size, which produces a per capita measure of welfare. This index is still very crude because all household members receive the same weight regardless of their age and sex and hence the per capita measure cannot capture income effects generated by economies of scale. Also, the per capita measure does not account for different consumption needs. Children consume less of certain goods than adults. A more elaborate description of the household is an equivalence scale, which assigns different consumption weights to household members of different age and sex. Those equivalence scales may be derived from expert opinion on how much a person of a certain age and sex ideally consumes. However, those expert based scales are subject to arbitrariness as virtual consumption patterns are not necessarily conform to expert nutritional recommendations and thus another approach is to estimate equivalence scales from observed behavior.

Such an approach is offered by the Engel method that has received wide attention in the recent empirical literature (among others Pendakur 1999, Yatchew et al. 2003). Using data from Belgian worker families, Engel observed that poorer households tend to spend a larger share of the household budget on food compared to richer families. This finding led him to the conclusion that the food share may be a good indicator of welfare (cited after Deaton (1997)), which is sometimes referred to as Engel's second law. According to this logic, households exhibiting a lower budget share on food are considered wealthier than households with a larger food share while households with the same share are treated as equally well off. One may use Engel's assertion to ask how much money we need to give to a larger household for it to achieve the same food share, i.e. the same welfare level, as a smaller household. In this regard, the demographic profile may be used to derive an index, or equivalence scale, that scales household welfare while holding the food share constant.

In practice, equivalence scales are derived from expenditure or cost functions where the equivalence scale $m(\cdot)$ serves to scale expenditure of a nonreference household such that it becomes equal to the expenditure of a reference household

$$c(p, u, a^N) = c(p, u, a^R) m(p, a^N) \tag{61}$$

where $a^R$ and $a^N$ denote the demographic profile of a reference and a non-reference household which may include information on household size, different ages and sex. $c(\cdot)$ is a cost function expressing the minimum amount of money needed to achieve utility $u$. Given prices $p$ and $u$ the cost function of the reference household is linearly scaled such that the equality holds. A convenient feature of the equivalence scale $m(p, a^N)$ is that it is independent of utility. This implies the strong assumption that the equivalence scale is the same across the whole range of expenditure levels. Rich households exhibit the same pattern of expenditure as compared to poor households, that is the Engel curves for reference and nonreference households are parallel. In the parlance of equivalence scale theory, this characteristic is called base-independence (Lewbel 1991) or equivalence scale exactness (Blackorby and Donaldson 1993).

Because utility is unobservable, it is more convenient to embed the equivalence scale in the dual indirect utility function to arrive at an estimable expression. This is possible since the homogeneity of degree one property of cost functions implies that the equivalence scale must be homogeneous of degree zero. Blackorby and Donaldson (1993) now start from expression (61) and construct an indirect utility function to express utility in terms of equivalent expenditure

$$\phi(p, x, a^N) = \phi\left(p, \frac{y}{m(p, a^N)}, a^R\right) \qquad (62)$$

where $y/m(p, a^N)$ is equivalent expenditure.

The estimation of equivalence scales is closely related to the estimation of Engel curves which relate the share of expenditure on a certain good to total outlay. The idea underlying the Engel method to compute equivalence scales is to compare households with differing demographic profiles but the same food budget shares. Figure 10 illustrates this relationship. The two curves denote food expenditure shares for two households (single adult ($S$) and one adult with a child ($L$)) of different sizes plotted against total expenditure. The curves are sloping downwards thus expressing the Engel law that expenditure shares on food decrease with rising levels of total expenditure. At expenditure level $x_0$, households $S$ and $L$ have different budget shares on food, implying that the large household is poorer given the same level of expenditure. Because at expenditure $x_0$ and $x_1$ both households have the same expenditure share for food, the difference between $x_0$ and $x_1$ is the amount of money needed to compensate the large household such that it achieves the same level of welfare as the small household. The equivalence scale is then given by $(x_1 - x_0)/x_0$.

The Engel method amounts to estimating the Engel curves—which can be derived from equation (62) using Roy's identity and multiplying the result by $p/y$ (see Pendakur 1999)—and to calculate the equivalence scale for each household type from the resulting parameters (see Deaton 1997). Although easy to implement, regarding the expenditure patterns of FHH and MHH, the Engel method may not be appropriate to identify the underlying equivalence scales. When extending the estimation of equivalence scales to include household characteristics other than household size and which seem to be irrelevant like the sex of the head of household, but which are associated with differing preferences for food, the usefulness of equivalence scales becomes doubtful. Different preferences would yield different demand patterns and ergo different equivalence scales for FHH and

## Figure 10: Identification of Engel equivalence scales

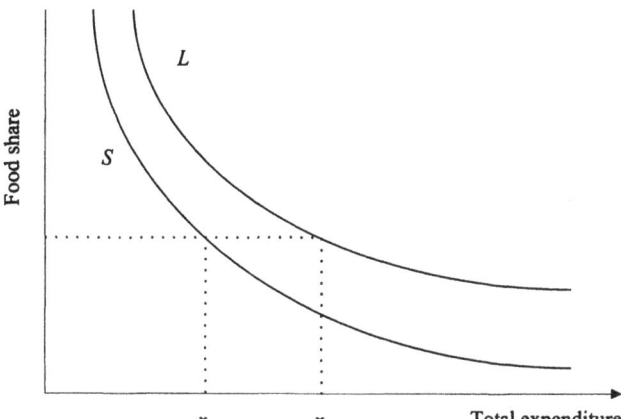

MHH. Drawing on the assertion that the food share serves as a welfare indicator, different food shares between FHH and MHH would then be interpreted as different levels of welfare which the households achieve. But this is not what equivalence scales want to express as higher food shares among FHH which are solely based on preferences render FHH poorer as MHH. If FHH reveal systematic differences in food demand which cannot be associated to household size, then identification of equivalence scales is clearly not free from utility as has been claimed in equation (61).

Similar criticisms have been brought forward by Deaton (1997) and Nicholson (1976) who doubt that the food share in the household budget is a sensible measure of welfare. The importance that food receives is dependent of the average welfare level of a given society. If the society is poor, then the primacy of food may be a plausible indicator of household welfare. In wealthier societies this may not be the case. Deaton further argues, that instead of relying on the food share one should rather focus on a more direct measure as nutritional status or individual food consumption.

The basic problem inherent to equivalence scales based on demand data is their dependence on preferences.[41] There is no reason to believe that preferences

---

[41] See also the critique by Pollak and Wales (1979) who doubt, that in general equivalence scales are identifiable using household demand data. Their argument rests on the assumption that children must be treated as consumption goods as well from which parents derive utility. Furthermore, parents deliberately choose their desired number of children, which according to Pollak and Wales renders welfare comparisons across families using equivalence scales meaningless. However, their argument does not necessarily apply to societies where fertility is a means of survival rather than a luxury. Family size in poor societies may therefore well be treated as exogenous. Furthermore, even when parents derive utility from children, the

regarding child welfare need to be the same across households with identical demographic profiles. As soon as behavior towards children which is partly reflected in household food demand differs systematically across households, equivalence scales immediately lose their meaning. To see this assume that demand data has been pooled, so that FHH and MHH are not explicitly distinguished.[42] Now form the ratio of the cost function of a reference and a nonreference household using (61) to get the equivalence scale for a household with profile $a^N$

$$m(p, a^N) = \frac{c(p, u, a^N)}{c(p, u, a^R)} \qquad (63)$$

Now as FHH and MHH are lumped together in these cost functions, one can write (63) equivalently in the form

$$m(p, a^N) = \frac{n_f}{n_f + n_m} \frac{c_f(p, u, a^N)}{c_f(p, u, a^R)} + \frac{n_m}{n_f + n_m} \frac{c_m(p, u, a^N)}{c_m(p, u, a^R)} \qquad (64)$$

Figure 11: Identification of Engel equivalence scales

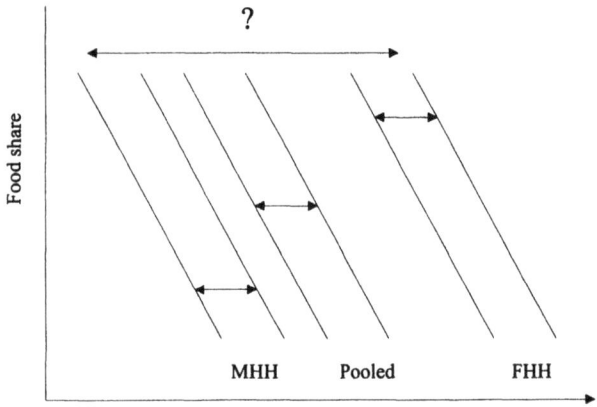

where the indexes $f$ and $m$ denote female and male heads of households, respectively, and $n$ is the number of households found in a particular category.

---

consumption needs still differ across families. When a family experiences an income shock, children may lose their status as being a 'consumption good', because family size is downwardly fixed and cannot be reduced.

[42]Note, that in this example, I focus on households where both, FHH and MHH, exhibit exactly the same demographic profile for the benchmark household. The comparison households have again the same household composition across household categories, but different from the benchmark.

It is obvious from this expression, that as soon the ratios of the cost functions $c_f(p,u,a^N)/c_f(p,u,a^R)$ and $c_m(p,u,a^N)/c_m(p,u,a^R)$ differ, the size of the equivalence scale is determined by the share of FHH in the society. This conclusion depends on the assumption of unequal ratios of the cost functions. As soon as the expenditure response to an additional child follows the same *relative* pattern across FHH and MHH, the size of the equivalence scale would not be affected.

However, even if the ratios were the same, it would only be possible to identify equivalence scales that serve as a useful guidance to compare expenditure behavior and welfare levels across households of the same headship category. But one cannot use such an equivalence scale to compare levels of welfare across FHH and MHH. This is illustrated in figure 11, where the parallel lines which are connected by an arrow represent food demand curves from households with a different demographic profile for each household category. From the pooled data, an equivalence scale—represented by the arrows—can be estimated that allows for a comparison of levels of welfare within each household category but not across. The equivalence scale that would be needed for that purpose is the one headed by the question mark whereas the difference between the within and across household category equivalence scales is obvious. In sum, the identification of a common equivalence scale that holds for comparisons of MHH and FHH is very unlikely from data where FHH and MHH have been pooled.

## 5.5 Difference of demand across FHH and MHH

The approach to estimate equivalence scales using semiparametric methods closely resembles the parametric approach embedded in a demand framework. In the first step, budget share equations (Engel curves) are estimated, one for each household with the $i$th demographic profile. In the second step, the average distance between the resulting demand curves is estimated, which gives the equivalence scales. The budget share equations are directly derived from the underlying utility model given in equation 62 (see Pendakur 1999). In the present application, instead of comparing households with different demographic profiles, I compare the demand curves of the two household categories FHH and MHH while controlling for the demographic profiles of each category. The demand model and the estimation procedure applied are the same as in the previous chapter, where for each household category a budget share equation was estimated of the form

$$w_{ij} = m(\ln(x_{ij})) + \alpha z_{ij} + \beta d_{ij} + \varepsilon_{ij} \qquad (65)$$

where the same variable definitions apply. Figure 12 repeats the demand curves for FHH and MHH as formerly presented in the previous chapter, which show the evolvement of demand for food with increasing expenditure while controlling for household characteristics. The difference between the curves casts doubt on the implicit assumption of any present approach to estimate equivalence scales that FHH and MHH form a homogeneous group generating the same demand curves. However, this assumption is the backbone for the identification of equivalence scales. The values indicating the scale and shift parameters between the curves indicate the statistical difference of the curves (see table 18 and discussion in chapter 4). Even the hypothesis that both curves exhibit the same shape is decisively rejected.

As the method pursued corresponds to the method for calculating equivalence scales as suggested by Pendakur (1999), Yatchew et al. (2003) and Stengos et al. (2006), the shift parameter can be interpreted as an equivalence scale. Consider equivalent expenditure of the form $x_i/a^N$. Taking logs of this expression yields $\ln x_i - \ln a^N$, which is equivalent to the expression in $m(\cdot)$ in equation 48. To obtain an equivalence scale between two household categories, one computes the distance between the expenditure levels of two households that exhibit the same food shares and this is precisely what the test based on equation (48) does. Assuming that equivalent expenditure between two different household categories can be written in the form

$$m(\ln x, \alpha^R) = m(\ln x - \alpha^N) + \eta^N \qquad (66)$$

where $R$ denotes a reference and $N$ a non-reference household, the shift parameter is equivalent to the equivalence scale $\alpha^{N}$[43]. For practical purposes, the procedure involves $\alpha^N = \ln a^N$, where $\alpha^N$ is a dummy variable representing FHH. Taking the antilog of $\alpha^N$ yields the equivalence scale $a^N$.

The estimated shift between the curves is $0.17$ $(0.037)$ and the scale parameter is estimated to be $0.041$ $(0.002)$, where the standard errors are given in parentheses. Taking the antilog of the estimated shift in order to arrive at the equivalence scale between MHH and FHH gives the value $1.19$. Therefore, to obtain the same level of welfare as a MHH given the same family size, a FHH needs to be compensated by $0.19$ times the expenditure of the MHH. This result is not in line with the Engel approach to equivalence scales, which aims at estimating general scales that are not specific to household characteristics other than the demographic profile. The estimates of the 'pseudo-equivalence scale' imply that systematically differing preferences across household categories cause the general equivalence scale estimates to be severely biased.[44]

---

[43] Pendakur (1999) interprets the scale parameter $\eta^N$ as a price elasticity of the equivalence scale. In his paper, he approximates $\eta^N$ by a variable denoting household size.

[44] It would be desirable to calculate the actual bias involved in the calculation of the cost of children. This would require to compare, say, households with two adults and no children with a family consisting of two adults and one child for each household category. However, given the heterogeneity of different demographic profiles in each category, there are not sufficient observations for each family type to render such calculations meaningful.

**Figure 12: Food budget shares for FHH and MHH**

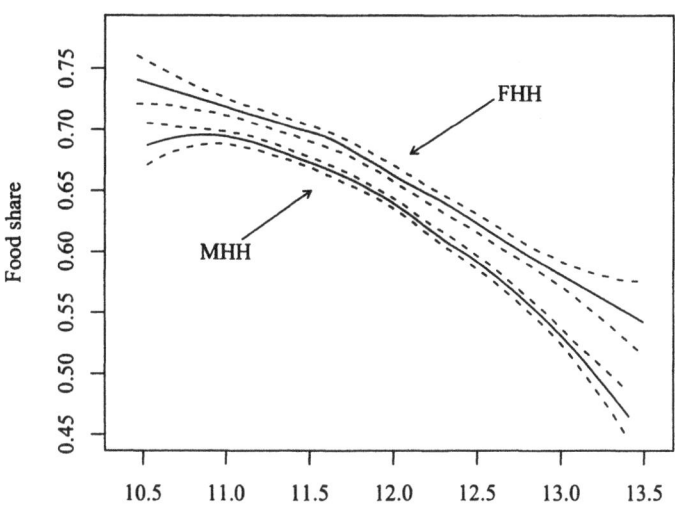

## 5.5 Food expenditure and children

Underlying the theory of Engel curve based equivalence scales is the assumption, that the calculation of an equivalence scale allows for identifying the cost of children. It is possible that although FHH spend more on food, the cost of an additional child is the same. To assess the different costs of children between FHH and MHH, we need to look at the parametric part of the model which is repeated here from the previous chapter.

The demographic composition parameters for children and juveniles reported in table 29 do not differ substantially from each other as most of them are not significant. Only the category boys of age 5 to 10 exhibits in MHH a significantly positive parameter while the category girls of age 11 to 15 is significant and negative in FHH. Thus it seems that child costs do not differ to a large extent between FHH and MHH. The adjustment of food expenditure in response to an additional household member is therefore largely driven by the household size parameter, which are negative and significant in both household categories. The parameter for FHH is smaller in absolute value, implying that an additional child causes a smaller reduction of per capita food spending compared to the adjustment within MHH. As an additional household member appears to reduce per

Table 29: Parameters of the semiparametric model - Food

|  | FHH | | MHH | |
| --- | --- | --- | --- | --- |
|  | Parameter | t-value | Parameter | t-value |
| ln Hhldsize | −0.048 ** | −12.656 | −0.063 ** | −24.197 |
| Boys 0-4 | −0.001 | −0.104 | 0.013 | 1.320 |
| Girls 0-4 | 0.006 | 0.405 | −0.000 | −0.037 |
| Boys 5-10 | 0.001 | 0.046 | 0.045 ** | 4.006 |
| Girls 5-10 | −0.006 | −0.436 | 0.018 | 1.593 |
| Boys 11-15 | −0.027 | −1.642 | −0.005 | −0.393 |
| Girls 11-15 | −0.031 ** | −2.039 | −0.020 | −1.511 |
| Male adults | −0.027 ** | −2.189 | −0.005 | −0.841 |
| Female adults | −0.039 ** | −4.516 | −0.012 ** | −1.484 |
| Primary education | −0.029 ** | −5.807 | −0.019 ** | −6.456 |
| Secondary education | −0.086 ** | −11.292 | −0.051 ** | −13.411 |
| Age | −0.000 | −0.094 | 0.000 ** | 4.713 |
| Rural | 0.029 ** | 6.722 | 0.029 ** | 11.754 |
| F | 20.346 | $p: 0.000$ | 59.491 | $p: 0.000$ |
| N | 4,737 | | 14,046 | |

** significant at 5 percent level

capita food spending,[45] expenditure on children is higher in that household, where the reduction in spending is lower. Given the smaller effect for FHH one may conclude that child welfare in FHH is higher, thus implying greater costs for children in FHH.

However, these estimates should be interpreted with caution because they imply a parallel scaling of the regression curve. Given the many facets that demand curves have in developing countries, the assumption of parallel demand curves for households of the same category but of different sizes and compositions may be too restrictive. To account for the possible nonparallelity, I compute regression curves for FHH and MHH by size and compare these curves to a common reference curve, for which FHH and MHH data have been pooled. All households are composed of two adults with varying numbers of children. Such a comparison bears nevertheless some problems as most FHH consist of mothers with children, that is, there is only a single adult. This holds true for 2,035 households of the FHH sample whereas only 1,382 FHH consist of two adults with children. However, I have chosen these compositions because the cells of the adult-children table are sparsely populated for single MHH with children. For example, only 84 MHH are single male adults with one child.

Figures 13 and 14 show the different nonparametric curves by household category. The thick line depicts the reference household (two adults and no children). In figure 14 it is striking that the curves are not parallel to each other and some exhibit even cubic shapes. Although these shapes may in part be determined by influential cases, the general trend of these curves is obvious: holding the per

---

[45]This finding has also been reported by Deaton and Paxson (1998) for huge variety of different countries.

capita total expenditure constant, the curves for FHH cluster closely around the reference curve while some even exceed the reference curve. In MHH, the picture is different: the curves exhibit a clear downscaling once the number of children is greater than zero. This is again contradictory to the assumption that food is an entirely private good that cannot be shared with others. The curves suggest that the degree of indivisibility of food is larger in FHH. An interesting feature of the two sets of curves is, that food shares within FHH first slightly decrease with an additional child. The household size is indicated by the arrows in the graph. When the number of children exceeds 3, the food shares start to rise again until they reach at the sixth child a level above the benchmark curve. Among MHH, the food shares constantly decline with an additional child, even though households with six children spent slightly more on food than households with five children.

Figure 13: Food budget shares for FHH of different sizes

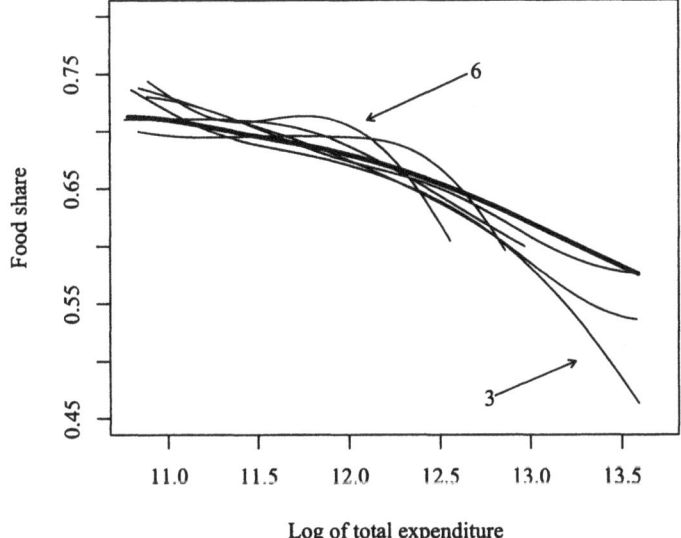

Log of total expenditure

## 5.5 Conclusions

The results presented here highlight the difficulties of estimating equivalence scales, when preferences differ systematically across households. Underlying the estimation of equivalence scales based on the Engel method is the assumption that preferences for food are only driven by household size. The results obtained show that such preferences are also influenced by other characteristics as the sex

Figure 14: Food budget shares for MHH of different sizes

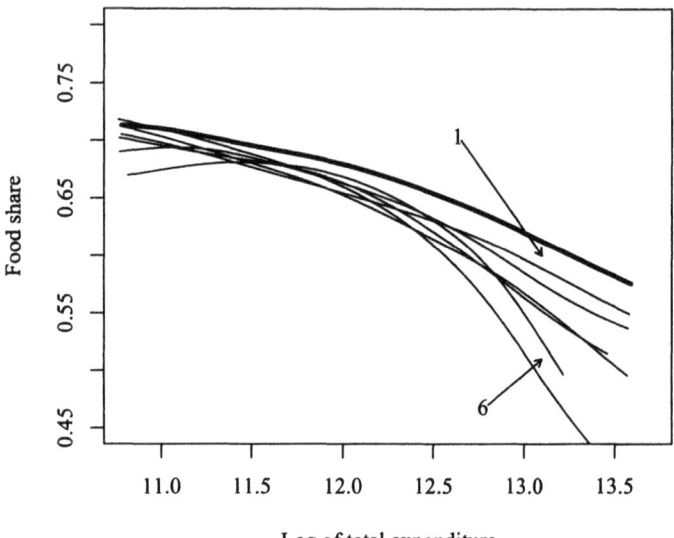

of the head of household. Interpreting the pseudo-equivalence scale leads to the conclusion that in order to achieve the same level of welfare, FHH need to be compensated by an income transfer of about 20 percent of a MHH, while holding the demographic profile constant. Whether this interpretation is meaningful is an open question, but it suggests that the Engel method of calculating equivalence scales contains a concept of utility that is not supported by empirical evidence. The comparison of food shares of different household categories is not sufficient to determine the real cost of a child which is obviously dependent on the preferences of the head of household.[46] As the results of this study show, the identification of any measure of equivalent income based on preferences may become severely biased if preferences differ significantly across individuals implying that expenditure is not determined by the household's demographic profile only.

Apart from Deaton's (1997) argument, who questions the adequacy of the food share to be an appropriate measure of welfare and asks whether alternative welfare measures such as nutritional status may be more appropriate, it is questionable whether there is *any* good that is free from preferences. The Engel method as well as other approaches based on goods demand as proposed by Barten (1964), Nicholson (1976), or Prais and Houthakker (1955) as well as the approach sug-

---

[46]Sen (1992) had similar reservations to the assumption that income translates equally into utility across different individuals.

gested by Rothbarth (as discussed in Deaton (1997)) suffer from the same problem. This difficulty also cannot be overcome by more sophisticated semiparametric approaches. In sum, the dependency of equivalence scales from preferences seem to invalidate this approach in general.

The choice of the category FHH and MHH is of course arbitrary and it is easy to think of other household characteristics that may bring about the same results. Other variables as educational background turned out to be significant in the demand functions as well. The impact of education on food demand thus renders the estimation of equivalence scales just as problematic as the differing preferences across FHH and MHH. Instead of equivalence scales one may rather speak of situation comparisons (Pollak and Wales 1979). Situation comparisons virtually build on the comparison of specific expenditure patterns conditional on prices and household size and do not measure the level of household welfare in terms of expenditure.

If the results presented here were to be interpreted as welfare measures, one would conclude that FHH are poorer than MHH because of their higher food shares. This is a strong assertion and renders welfare measures generally sensitive to the choice of equivalence scale. If scales based on food demand were to be used, FHH would always become poorer compared to a welfare per capita measure. The differences of demand behavior also relate to the calculation of food consumption baskets, which are used to set poverty lines. The poverty line and thus the poverty rate of a society may face substantial changes whether food consumption is based on data from FHH or MHH. With more FHH in the sample, the poverty rate would increase.

In view of these difficulties, the usage of a uni-dimensional indicator of welfare is as such questionable. As Klasen (2000) has shown, there are serious problems to efficiently target poverty reduction programs if targeting is built on an expenditure based measure of welfare only. The comparison of a consumption measure with another constructed on deprivation data yielded substantial differences regarding the size and composition of the groups considered as poor. The findings presented in this chapter further support the application of multi-dimensional measures of welfare that extend to access and quality of education, housing, water or sanitation among others.

# 6 Summary and conclusions

This study focuses on two questions: (i) what are the implications of differing preferences and constraints across gender for economic behavior and the measurement of welfare and (ii) how are structural conditions reflected in women's preferences and behavior. The results reveal that gender inequality plays a role in determining household decisions and production outcomes. In the first chapter it was shown that tenure insecurity of FHH and women's low on-farm decision capabilities lead to lower productivity. The results further support the assumption that preferences differ across gender. The investigation of fertility decisions in the framework of an intrahousehold bargaining model yielded that the number of a couple's children significantly decreases with increasing female bargaining power. However, the same conclusion does not hold regarding birth spacing. Also, I examined spending behavior of FHH and find that FHH spend significantly more on food and child welfare compared with MHH. Finally using this information for investigating the possibility to identify equivalence scales from demand data, I conclude that measures involving preferences do not yield meaningful results on the welfare of individuals and households.

Regarding the second aim of the study, it was assumed that the observation of behavioral differences depends on the state in which households are. The state refers either to the surrounding institutional environment or to personal perceptions. The perceptions that are investigated in the second chapter relate to the individual assessment of income risks. The empirical results point to the possibility that such state dependency does indeed exist. Certain categories of FHH turn out to be more productive than MHH when facing the risk of income shortfalls although being subject to tenure insecurity and low decision power. However, the same household categories shift into another state which is associated with lower income risk, if off-farm incomes are available. In this state, the negative effects from tenure insecurity and low decision power are eventually becoming obvious.

The results in the third chapter support the assumption that preferences are state dependent as well, that is, determined by gender inequality regarding access to old age security. Differing preferences therefore may not be directly grounded in gender as such but might have structural reasons. Since food demand of FHH decreases to the level of MHH once savings are introduced into the demand equation, the conclusion that women generally spend more money on food and child welfare may need to be reconsidered.

Such reconsideration includes explicitly taking the constraints of women into account in any analysis of preferences and behavior. The results of such an extended analysis may reveal that some of the reasons why women act differently from men can be explained through rational behavior. That is, due to their exposition to, e.g., different institutional constraints, women and men may rationally respond to incentives given by the surrounding institutional environment.

The importance of considering the differential institutional setting became obvious in the second chapter, where the institutional environment on the one hand, and the perception of risk on the other hand determined the productive outcomes of households. Without explicit consideration of these two factors, generating the empirical result would not have been possible.

Simple demand analysis thus falls short of uncovering gender differences in preferences if being a female consumer implies that preferences are shaped by deprivation. In the case presented in chapter four, this is given by lacking access to the insurance market for old age security. However, behavioral differences may disappear once the economic and social environment changes. In the example scrutinized here, the improvement of insurance markets may be followed by a reduction of food demand among FHH. However, further analysis of the impact of institutional settings on patterns of spending would be required to fully understand the (dynamic) relationship between spending and savings. Comparing countries with different social safety systems and examining behavioral outcomes like spending on children would reveal deeper insights into the old age security hypothesis. Similar considerations hold for the different fertility preferences of women and men. If lower preferences for fertility as expressed by women depend on the costs that child bearing incurs, changing these costs may affect the desired number of children as well. The health system is an important factor in this regard, as with improved pre- and postnatal health care, the health risks borne by women decline, thus implying a reduction of costs which may induce a rise in the number of desired children.

The analysis of gender differences should therefore not stop at finding such differences, but engage in examining the underlying causes. It is important in this regard, to consider that preferences are not static and change over time. It is often argued that female labor market participation reduces fertility. However, whether this effect stems from an improvement of bargaining power or from changing attitudes towards the quantity and quality of children is unclear. Increased education of women and improved access to labor markets, credits and productive resources, as well as the dissemination of contraceptives may induce changes of preferences through creating new opportunities. Incorporating such considerations into future research is likely to bring about important results, which would help to improve existing policies and to facilitate the design of new initiatives to support women and simultaneously spur the process of development.

As yet, the discussion primarily focused on preferences which are brought about by gender inequality. However, gender inequality itself is not only rooted in traditions, but may also have economic reasons. An example is provided by the theory on the emergence of different marriage systems involving bride price and polygamy. (Boserup 1970) and (Goody 1973) claim that due to different agricultural production systems different value is attached to female labor. Where substantial labor is needed for agricultural production as in hand hoe dominated systems, bride prices and polygamy prevail. In this example, social norms that result into gender inequality arise from different natural environments that are exogenous to the society, but might be influenced by technological change. If these channels through which gender inequality arises are well understood, development policies are likely to be much more efficient.

The results presented here also point to the fact that the standard methods and tools commonly applied to analyze gender issues are not always appropriate to discover the underlying causes of behavioral differences or preferences. For example, standard quantitative methods may fall short of fully accounting for the multidimensional concept of bargaining power. The incorporation of a set of variables measuring bargaining power alleviates the difficulties, but the variables included can only be considered as crude approximations. Therefore, carefully reviewing the local culture and institutions is necessary to conduct research of the intrahousehold bargaining process in particular and gender issues in general. However, the inclusion of assets brought to marriage has been found to reveal very similar results across different countries and may thus be considered as a robust indicator of bargaining power (see Maluccio and Quisumbing 1999).

Moreover, as the analysis in the final chapter has shown, differing preferences across gender have also implications for methods aiming at generating measures that allow for welfare comparisons across households. The identification of poor women is aggravated by inappropriate means to account for household demographics in the comparison of welfare across individuals and households. Measures implicitly assuming that utility derived from certain goods is the same across all individuals, regardless of their gender, fail to provide deeper insights into subjective wellbeing. Beyond gender, other characteristics like age, culture or geographical location significantly influence preferences as well. This result puts into question the robustness of different welfare measures to the choice of the underlying model of utility. However, the results from the previous chapters also emphasize that such preferences may not be static. If women and men principally have similar preference structures, rendered different by different constraints, then adjusting the existing methods to the constraints may help in improving their meaningfulness.

Regarding research on causes for differing preferences and gender inequality, research on gender issues in economics seems to be still in its infancy. Very few papers strive for explaining the underlying causes of differing preferences for child welfare beyond *ad hoc* rationalizations of observed behavior. Furthermore, the explanations provided largely remain untested. The same holds for gender inequality, for which not much is known about possible economic reasons. Such complex relations are, however, a topic of its own and not yet sufficiently addressed in the current literature on gender.

# References

Amemiya, T. 1985. *Advanced Econometrics*, Basil Blackwell, Oxford.

Andres, L. and Urzua, S. 2003. New evidence on the relationship between fertility spacing and economic variables, *mimeo*.

Anim, F. 1999. A note on the adoption of soil conservation measures in the Northern Province of South Africa, *Journal of Agricultural Economics* 50(2): 336–345.

Anker, R. and Knowles, J. 1982. *Fertility differentials in developing countries. A case study of Kenya*, Ordina, Liege.

Arnstein, A. and Altankhuyag, G. 2001. Changing pattern of fertility behavior in a time of social and economic change: evidence from Mongolia, *Working paper 2001-023*, Max Planck Institute for Demographic Research.

Arroyo, C. R. and Zhang, J. 1997. Dynamic microeconomic models of fertility choice: A survey, *Journal of Population Economics* 10(1): 23–65.

Bankole, A. and Singh, S. 1998. Couples' fertility and contraceptive decision-making in developing countries: Hearing the man's voice, *International Family Planning Perspectives* 24(1): 15–24.

Barbier, B. 1998. Induced innovation and land degradation: Results from a bioeconomic model of a village in West Africa, *Agricultural Economics* 19(1-2): 15–21.

Barten, A. 1964. Family composition, prices and expenditure patterns, *in* P. Hart and G. Mills (eds), *Econometric Analysis for National Economic Planning*, 16th Symposium of the Colston Society, Butterworth, London.

Beegle, K., Frankenberg, E. and Thomas, D. 2001. Bargaining power within couples and use of prenatal and delivery care in Indonesia, *Studies in Family Planning* 32(2): 130–146.

Behrman, J. and Deolalikar, A. 1987. Will developing country nutrition improve with rising income? A case study for rural South India, *Journal of Political Economy* 95(3): 492–507.

Behrman, J. R. 1997. Intrahousehold distribution and the family, *in* M. R. Rosenzweig and O. Stark (eds), *Handbook of Population and Family Economics*, Vol. 1 of *Handbook of Population and Family Economics*, Elsevier, chapter 4, pp. 125–187.

Behrman, J., Sengupta, P. and Todd, P. 2005. Progressing with PROGRESA: An impact assessment of a school subsidy experiment in rural Mexico, *Economic Development and Cultural Change* **54**(1): 237–275.

Benefo, K. and Schultz, T. P. 1996. Fertility and child mortality in Côte d'Ivoire and Ghana, *World Bank Economic Review* **10**(1): 123–58.

Besley, T. 1995. Property rights and investment incentives: Theory and evidence from Ghana, *Journal of Political Economy* **103**(5): 903–937.

Bhalotra, S. and Attfield, C. 1998. Intrahousehold resource allocation in rural Pakistan: A semiparametric analysis, *Journal of Applied Econometrics* **13**(5): 463–480.

Bindlish, V. and Evenson, R. E. 1993. Evaluation of the performance of T&V extension in Kenya, *World Bank Technical Paper No. 208, Africa Technical Department Series*, World Bank, Washington, D.C.

Bindlish, V., Evenson, R. E. and Gbetibouo, M. 1993. Evaluation of T&V based extension in Burkina Faso, *World Bank Technical Paper No. 226, Africa Technical Department Series*, World Bank, Washington, D.C.

Blackden, M. and Bhanu, C. 1999. Gender, growth and poverty reduction, *World Bank Technical Papers 428*, Special Programme of Assistance for Africa, 1988 Status Report on Poverty, World Bank, Washington DC.

Blackden, M., Canagarajah, S., Klasen, S. and Lawson, D. 2006. Gender and growth in sub-Saharan Africa. Issues and evidence, *Research Paper, No. 2006/37*, UNU-WIDER.

Blackorby, C. and Donaldson, D. 1993. Adult equivalence scales and the economic implementation of interpersonal comparisons of well-being, *Social Choice and Welfare* **10**: 335–361.

Bloom, D. E. and Williamson, J. G. 1998. Demographic transitions and economic miracles in emerging asia, *World Bank Economic Review* **12**(3): 419–456.

Blundell, R., Duncan, A. and Pendakur, K. 1998. Semiparametric estimation and consumer demand, *Journal of Applied Econometrics* **13**(5): 435–461.

Bongaarts, J. 1985. Measuring wanted fertility, *Population and Development Review* **37**(3): 513–534.

Boserup, E. 1970. *Women's role in economic development*, St. Martin's Press, New York.

Browning, M., Bourguignon, F., Chiappori, P.-A. and Lechene, V. 1994. Incomes and outcomes: A structural model of intrahousehold allocation, *Journal of Political Economy* **102**(6): 1067–1096.

Browning, M. and Chiappori, P.-A. 1998. Efficient intra-household resource allocations: a general characterization and empirical tests, *Econometrica* **66**(6): 1241–1278.

Bruce, J. 1989. Homes divided, *World Development* **17**(7): 979–992.

Bruce, J. and Migot-Adholla, S. 1994. *Searching for land tenure security in Africa*, Kendall/ Hunt Publishing Co., Dubuque.

Cain, M. 1981. Risk and insurance: Perspecties on fertility and agrarian change in India and Bangladesh, *Population and Development Review* **7**(3): 435–474.

Cain, M. 1982. Perspectives on family and fertility in developing countries, *Population and Development Review* **36**(2): 159–175.

Cain, M. 1983. Fertility as an adjustment to risk, *Population and Development Review* **9**(4): 688–702.

Caldwell, J. C. 1986. Routes to low mortality in poor countries, *Population and Development review* **12**(2): 171–220.

Camerer, C., Babcock, L., Loewenstein, G. and Thaler, R. 1997. Labor supply of New York city cab drivers: One day at a time?, *Quarterly Journal of Economics* **112**: 407–441.

Cameron, A. C. and Trivedi, P. K. 1998. *Regression analysis of count data*, Cambridge University Press, Cambridge.

Chiappori, P.-A. 1988. Rational household labor supply, *Econometrica* **56**(1): 63–90.

Chiappori, P.-A. 1992. Collective labor supply and welfare, *Journal of Political Economy* **100**(3): 437–467.

Chipande, C. 1987. Innovation adoption among female-headed households, *Development and Change* **18**(2): 315–328.

Christensen, L., Jorgenson, D. and Lau, L. J. 1971a. Conjugate duality and the transcendental logarithmic production function, *Econometrica* **39**(4): 255–256.

Christensen, L., Jorgenson, D. and Lau, L. J. 1971b. Transcendental logarithmic production frontiers, *Review of Economics and Statistics* **55**(1): 28–45.

Christensen, L., Jorgenson, D. and Lau, L. J. 1974. Transcendental logarithmic utility function, *American Economic Review* **65**: 267–383.

Cigno, A. 1993. Intergenerational transfers without altruism. Family, market and state, *European Journal of Political Economy* **9**: 505–518.

Cleveland, W. 1979. Robust locally weighted regression and smoothing scatterplots, *Journal of the American Statistical Association* **74**: 829–836.

Cragg, J. 1971. Some statistical models for limited dependent variables with application to the demand of durable goods, *Econometrica* **39**: 829–844.

Dalton, T. J., Masters, W. A. and Foster, K. A. 1997. Production costs and input substitution in Zimbabwe's smallholder agriculture, *Agricultural Economics* **17**: 201–209.

Davison, J. 1988. Who owns what? Land registration and tensions in gender relations of production in Kenya, *in* J. Davison (ed.), *Agriculture, women and land: The African experience*, Westview, Boulder.

Deaton, A. 1997. *The analysis of household surveys. A microeconometric approach to development policy*, Johns Hopkins University Press, Baltimore.

Deaton, A. and Paxson, C. 1998. Economies of scale, household size, and the demand for food, *Journal of Political Economy* **106**(5): 897–930.

Deaton, A., Ruiz-Castillo, J. and Thomas, D. 1989. The influence of household composition on household expenditure patterns: Theory and Spanish evidence, *Journal of Political Economy* **97**(1): 179–200.

Dempster, A., Laird, N. and Rubin, D. 1977. Maximum likelihood from incomplete data via the EM algorithm, *Journal of the Royal Statistical Society, Series B* **39**(1): 1–38.

Dodoo, F. 1992. Men matter: additive and interactive gendered preferences and reproductive behavior in Kenya, *Demography* **35**(2): 229–242.

Donaldson, D. and Pendakur, K. 2005. Equivalence scales with fixed costs of characteristics, *Discussion Paper 05-09*, University of British Columbia, Department of Economics.

Doornik, J. A. 2002. *Object-oriented matrix programming using Ox*, 3 edn, Timberlake Consultants Press, London.

Doss, C. 2001. Designing agricultural technologies for African women farmers: lessons from 25 years of experience, *World Development* **29**(12): 2075–2092.

Doss, C. and Morris, M. L. 2001. How does gender affect the adoption of agricultural innovations? The case of improved maize technology in Ghana, *Agricultural Economics* 25(1): 27–39.

Doss, C. R. 1996. Do Households Fully Share Risk? Evidence From Ghana, *Staff Papers 96-10*, University of Minnesota, Department of Applied Economics.

Drèze, J. and Srinivasan, P. 1997. Widowhood and poverty in rural India: Some inferences from household survey data, *Journal of Development Economics* 54: 217–234.

Duflo, E. and Udry, C. 2004. Intrahousehold resource allocation in Côte d'Ivoire: Social norms, separate accounts and consumption choices, *NBER Working Papers 10498*, National Bureau of Economic Research, Inc.

Dyson, T. and Moore, M. 1983. On kinship structure, female autonomy, and demographic behavior in India, *Population and Development Review* 9: 35–60.

Ebert, U. 1997. Social welfare when needs differ: an axiomatic approach, *Economica* 64: 233–244.

Ebert, U. and Moyes, P. 2003. Equivalence scales reconsidered, *Econometrica* 71: 319–343.

Ellis, A., Blackden, M., Cutura, J., MacCulloch, F. and Seebens, H. 2007. *Gender and economic growth in Tanzania: creating opportunities for women*, Directions in Development. Private Sector Development, The World Bank, Washington DC.

Eswaran, M. 2002. The empowerment of women, fertility, and child mortality: Towards a theoretical analysis, *Journal of Population Economics* 15: 433–454.

Evenson, R. E. and Mwabu, G. 1998. The effects of agricultural extension on farm yields in Kenya, *Center Discussion Paper No. 798*, Economic Growth Center, Yale University.

Famoye, F. 1993. A restricted generalized Poisson regression model, *Communications in Statistics - Theory and Methods* 22: 1335–1354.

Famoye, P. C. F. 1992. A generalized Poisson regression model, *Communications in Statistics - Theory and Method* 21: 89–109.

Farber, H. S. 2005. Is tomorrow another day? The labor supply of New York city cab drivers, *Journal of Political Economy* 22: 1335–1354.

Feder, G., Just, R. E. and Zilberman, D. 1988. Adoption of agricultural innovations in developing countries: A survey, *Economic Development and Cultural Change* 33(2): 255–298.

Finkelshtain, I. and Chalfant, J. A. 1991. Marketed surplus under risk: Do peasants agree with Sandmo?, *American Journal of Agricultural Economics* pp. 557–567.

Forson, G. B. 1999. Factors influencing adoption of land-enhancing technology in the Sahel: Lessons from a case study in Niger, *Agricultural Economics* 20(3): 231–239.

Fortin, B. and Lacroix, G. 1997. A test of the unitary and collective models of household labour supply, *Economic Journal* 107: 933–955.

Fuss, M., McFadden, D. and Mundlak, Y. 1978. A survey of functional forms in the economic analysis of production, *in* M. Fuss and D. McFadden (eds), *Production economics: A dual approach to theory and applications*, North-Holland, Amsterdam.

Fuwa, N. 2000. A note on the analysis of female headed households in developing countries, *The Technical Bulletin of the Faculty of Horticulture 54*, Chiba University.

Goffe, W. L., Ferrier, G. D. and Rogers, J. 1994. Global optimization of statistical functions with simulated annealing, *Journal of Econometrics* 60(1-2): 65–99.

Goldstein, M. 1999. 'Chop time, no friends'. Intrahousehold and individual insurance mechanisms in southern Ghana. mimeo.

Goody, J. 1973. Bridewealth and dowry in Africa and Eurasia, *in* J. Goody and S. J. Tambiah (eds), *Bridewealth and dowry*, Cambridge University press, Cambridge.

Gopal, G. and Salim, M. 1998. *Gender and law. Eastern Africa speaks*, The World Bank, Washington DC.

Gorman, W. M. 1981. Some engel curves, *in* A. Deaton (ed.), *Essays in Honour of Sir Richard Stone*, Johns Hopkins University Press, Cambridge, pp. 1–10.

Gozalo, P. 1997. Nonparametric bootstrap analysis with applications to demographic effects in demand functions, *Journal of Econometrics* 81: 357–393.

Griliches, Z. and Mairesse, J. 1998. Production functions: the search for identification, *in* Z. Griliches (ed.), *Practicing Econometrics: Essays in Methods and Applications*, Edward Elgar, pp. 383–411.

Haddad, L. 1999. The earned income by women: impacts on welfare outcomes, *Agricultural Economics* **20**: 135–141.

Haddad, L. and Hoddinott, J. 1994. Women's income and boy-girl anthropometric Status in the Côte D'Ivoire, *World Development* **22**(4): 543–553.

Halvorsen, R. and Palmquist, R. 1980. The interpretation of dummy variables in semilogarithmic equations, *American Economic Review* **70**: 474–475.

Handa, S. 1994. Gender, headship, and intra-household resource allocation, *World Development* **22**(10): 1535–1547.

Handa, S. 1996a. Expenditure behavior and children's welfare: An analysis of female headed households in Jamaica, *Journal of Development Economics* **50**: 165–187.

Handa, S. 1996b. The determinants of female headship in Jamaica: Results from a structural model, *Economic Development and Cultural Change* pp. 793–815.

Härdle, W. and Marron, J. 1990. Semiparametric comparison of regression curves, *Annals of Statistics* **18**(1): 63–89.

Härdle, W., Müller, M., Sperlich, S. and Werwatz, A. 2004. *Nonparametric and semiparametric models*, Springer, Berlin.

Hausman, J. 1978. Specification tests in econometrics, *Econometrica* **646**: 1251–1271.

Heady, E. O. and Dillon, J. L. 1961. *Agricultural production functions*, Iowa University Press, Ames, Iowa.

Heckman, J. 1976. The common structure of statistical models of truncation, sample selection and limited dependent variables and a simple estimator for such models, *Annals of Economic and Social Measurement* **5**: 475–492.

Heckman, J. 1979. Sample selection bias as a specification error, *Econometrica* **1**: 153–161.

Heckman, J. J. and Walker, J. R. 1987. Using goodness of fit and other criteria to choose among competing duration models: A case study of Hutterite data, *Sociological Methodology* **17**: 247–307.

Heckman, J. J. and Walker, J. R. 1990a. The relationship between wages and income and the timing and spacing of births: evidence from Swedish longitudinal data, *Econometrica* **58**(6): 1411–41.

Heckman, J. J. and Walker, J. R. 1990b. The third birth in Sweden, *Journal of Population Economics* **3**(4): 235–75.

Heckman, J. and Singer, B. 1984. A method for minimizing the impact of distributional assumptions in econometric models for duration data, *Econometrica* **52**(2): 271–320.

Hoddinott, J. and Haddad, L. 1995. Does Female Income Share Influence Household Expenditures? Evidence from Côte d'Ivoire, *Oxford Bulletin of Economics and Statistics* **57**(1): 77–96.

Hogan, D. P., Berhanu, B. and Hailemariam, A. 1999. Household organization, women's autonomy, and contraceptive behavior in Southern Ethiopia, *Studies in Family Planning* **30**(4): 302–314.

Hotz, J., Klerman, V., Alex, J. and Willis, R. J. 1993. The economics of fertility in developed countries, *in* M. R. Rosenzweig and O. Stark (eds), *Handbook of Population and Family Economics*, Vol. 1 of *Handbook of Population and Family Economics*, Elsevier, chapter 7, pp. 275–347.

Huber, P. 1967. The behavior of maximum likelihood estimates under nonstandard conditions, *Proceedings of the Fifth Berkeley Symposium on Mathematical Statistics and Probability*, University California Press, Berkeley, pp. 221–233.

Jacoby, H. 1993. Shadow wages and peasant labor supply: An econometric application to the Peruvian Sierra, *Review of Economic Studies* **60**: 901–921.

Jorgenson, D. 1986. Econometric methods for modeling producer behavior, *in* Z. Griliches and M. Intriligator (eds), *Handbook of Econometrics*, Vol. 3, Elsevier, chapter 31, pp. 1841–1915.

Kello, A. B. and Papagallo, S. 1997. The health sector review: the regional report, *in* Ministry of Finance (ed.), *Social Sector Review*, Vol. 2, Federal Democratic Republic of Ethiopia, chapter 2, pp. 79–108.

Kennedy, E. and Peters, P. 1992. Household food security and child nutrition: the interaction of income and gender of the household head, *World Development* **20**(8): 1077–1085.

Kennedy, P. 1981. Estimation with correctly interpreted dummy variables in semilogarithmic equations, *American Economic Review* **71**: 801.

Klasen, S. 2000. Measuring poverty and deprivation in South Africa, *Review of Income and Wealth* **46**(1): 33–58.

Klasen, S. 2002. Low schooling for girls, slower growth for all?, *World Bank Economic Review* **16**: 345–73.

Klasen, S. and Lamanna, F. 2003. The impact of gender inequality in education and employment on economic growth in the Middle East and North Africa. mimeo.

Klasen, S. and Launov, A. 2006. Analysis of the determinants of fertility decline in the Czech Republic, *Journal of Population Economics* 19(1): 25–54.

Kumbhakar, A. and Lovell, C. 2000. *Stochastic frontier analysis*, Cambridge University Press, Cambridge.

Lapar, M. L. and Pandey, S. 1999. Adoption of soil conservation: The case of the Philippine uplands, *Agricultural Economics* 21(3): 241–256.

Lawrence Haddad, J. H. and Alderman, H. 1997. *Intrahousehold resource allocation in developing countries. Models, methods and policies*, Johns Hopkins University Press, Baltimore.

Leroux, B. G. 1992. Consistent estimation of a mixture distribution, *Annals of Statistics* 20(3): 1350–1360.

Lesperance, M. and Lindsay, B. 2001. Statistical computing in mixture models, *Technical Report 01-07-13*, Pennstate University, Department of Statistics.

Lewbel, A. 1991. Cost of characteristics indices and household equivalence scales, *European Economic Review* 36: 1277–1293.

Lindstrom, D. P. and Berhanu, B. 1999. The impact of war, famine and economic decline on marital fertility in Ethiopia, *Demography* 36(2): 247–261.

Lundberg, S. and Pollak, R. A. 1993. Separate spheres bargaining and the marriage market, *Journal of Political Economy* 101(6): 988–1010.

Maddala, G. 1983. *Limited-dependent and qualitative variables in econometrics*, Cambridge University Press, Cambridge.

Maluccio, J. and Quisumbing, A. 1999. Intrahousehold allocation and gender relations: New empirical evidence, *Policy Research Report on Gender and Development, Working Paper Series 2*, World Bank.

Manser, M. and Brown, M. 1980. Marriage and household decision-making: A bargaining analysis, *International Economic Review* 21(1): 31–44.

Marcel Fafchamps, A. d. J. and Sadoulet, E. 1991. Peasant household behavior with missing markets: some paradoxes explained, *Economic Journal* 101: 1851–1868.

Mason, K. and Taj, A. M. 1987. Differences between women's and men's reproductive goals in developing countries, *Population and Development Review* 13: 611–638.

McElroy, M. B. and Horney, M. J. 1981. Nash-bargained household decisions: Toward a generalization of the theory of demand, *International Economic Review* 22(2): 333–349.

McLachlan, G. and Peel, D. 2000. *Finite mixture models*, Wiley, New York.

Menon, M., Perali, F. and Rosati, F. 2005. The shadow wage of child labour: An application to Nepal, *UCW Working Paper 11*, Understanding Children's Work (UCW Project).

Mesfin, G. 2002. The role of men in fertility and family planning program in Tigray region, *Ethiopian Journal of Health Development* 16(3): 247–255.

Migot-Adholla, S., Hazell, P., Blarel, B. and Place, F. 1991. Indigenous land rights systems in Sub-Saharan Africa: A constraint of productivity?, *World Bank Economic Review* 3(1): 155–175.

Minot, N., Kherallah, M. and Berry, P. 2000. Fertilizer market liberalization in Benin and Malawi. A household level view. mimeo.

Moock, P. 1976. The efficiency of women as farm managers: Kenya, *American Journal of Agricultural Economics* 58(5): 831–835.

Murthi, M., Guio, A.-C. and Drèze, J. 1995. Mortality, fertility, and gender bias in India: A district level analysis, *Population and Development Review* 21: 745–782.

Newman, J. L. and McCulloch, C. E. 1984. A hazard rate approach to the timing of births, *Econometrica* 52(4): 939–961.

Nicholson, L. J. 1976. Appraisal of different methods of estimating equivalence scales and their results, *Econometrica* 22: 1–11.

Nugent, J. 1985. The old age security motive for having children, *Population and Development Review* 11(1): 75–98.

Nugent, J. B. and Gillaspy, T. R. 1983. Old age pensions and fertility in rural areas of less developed countries: Some evidence from Mexico, *Economic Development and Cultural Change* 31(4): 809–829.

P. Hall, J. K. and Titterington, D. 1990. Asymptotically optimal difference based estimation of variance in nonparametric regression, *Biometrika* 77: 521–528.

Pendakur, K. 1999. Estimates and tests of base-independent equivalence scales, *Journal of Econometrics* **88**(1): 1–40.

Pender, J. L. and Kerr, J. 1998. Determinants of farmersŠ indigenous soil and water conservation investments in semi-arid India, *Agricultural Economics* **19**(1-2): 113–125.

Pollak, R. A. and Wales, T. J. 1979. Welfare comparisons and equivalence scales, *American Economic Review* **69**(2): 216–221.

Population Reference Bureau 2004. World Population Data Sheet.

Prais, S. and Houthakker, H. 1955. *The analysis of family budgets*, Cambridge University Press, Cambridge.

Pritchett, L. 1994. Desired fertility and the impact of population policies, *Population and Development Review* **20**(1): 1–55.

Quisumbing, A. (ed.) 2003. *Household decisions, gender, and development. A synthesis of recent research*, International Food Policy Research Institute, Washington DC.

Quisumbing, A. and Maluccio, J. 2000. Intrahousehold allocation and gender relations: new empirical evidence from four developing countries, *FCND Discussion Paper No. 84*, International Food Policy Research Institute (IFPRI), Washington D.C.

Rilstone, P. and Ullah, A. 1989. Nonparametric estimation of response coefficients, *Communications in Statistics, Theory and Methods* **18**: 669–680.

Robinson, P. 1988. Root-n-consistent semiparametric regression, *Econometrica* **56**: 931–954.

Rogers, B. L. 1995. The implications of female household headship for food consumption and nutritional status in the Dominican Republic, *World Development* **24**(1): 113–128.

Rosenhouse, S. 1989. Identifying the poor: Is 'headship' a useful concept?, *Living Standard Measurement Working Paper 58*, World Bank.

Ruppert, D., Wand, M. and Carroll, R. J. 2003. *Semiparametric Regression*, Cambridge University Press, Cambridge.

Saito, K., Mekonnen, H. and Spurling, D. 1994. Raising the productivity of women farmers in sub-Saharan Africa, *World Bank Africa Technical Department Series 230 230*, World Bank, Washington D.C.

Saito, K. and Weidemann, C. J. 1990. Agricultural extension for women farmers in africa, *World Bank Africa Discussion Papers 103*, World Bank, Washington D.C.

Sandmo, A. 1971. On the theory of the competitive firm under price uncertainty, *American Economic Review* **61**: 65–73.

Savane, M. A. 1986. The effects of social and economic changes on the role and status of women in sub-Saharan Africa, in J. L. Moock (ed.), *Understanding Africa's Rural Households and Farming Systems*, Westview Press, Boulder, pp. 125–132.

Schäfer, R. 2002. Gender und ländliche Entwicklung in Afrika, *Aus Politik und Zeitgeschichte*, Bundeszentrale für politische Bildung.

Schultz, T. P. 1993. Demand for children in low income countries, in M. R. Rosenzweig and O. Stark (eds), *Handbook of Population and Family Economics*, Vol. 1 of *Handbook of Population and Family Economics*, Elsevier, chapter 8, pp. 349–430.

Sen, A. 1997. Population policy: Authoritarianism versus cooperation, *Journal of Population Economics* **10**(1): 3–22.

Sen, A. K. 1992. *Inequality re-examind*, Harvard University Press, Cambridge.

Shively, G. 1997. Consumption risk, farm characteristics, and soil conservation adoption, *Agricultural Economics* **17**: 165–177.

Shonkwiler, J. and Yen, S. 1999. Two-step estimation of a censored system of equations, *American Journal of Agricultural Economics* **81**(4): 972–982.

Short, S. and Kiros, G.-E. 2002. Husbands, wives, sons, and daughters: Fertility preferences and the demand for contraception in Ethiopia, *Population Research and Policy Review* **21**(5): 377–402.

Sibanda, A., Woubalem, Z., Hogan, D. P. and Lindstrom, D. P. 2003. The proximate determinants of the decline to below replacement fertility in Addis Ababa, Ethiopia, *Studies of Family Planning* **34**(1): 1–7.

Skoufias, E. 1994. Using shadow wages to estimate labor supply of agricultural households, *American Journal of Agricultural Economics* **76**: 331–339.

Speckman, P. 1988. Kernel smoothing in partial linear models, *Journal of the Royal Statistical Society, B* **50**: 413–436.

Stengos, T., Sun, Y. and Wang, D. 2006. Estimates of semiparametric equivalence scales, *Journal of Applied Econometrics* **21**(5): 629–639.

Tauchmann, H. 2005. Efficiency of two-step estimators for censored systems of equations: Shonkwiler and Yen reconsidered, *Applied Economics* **37**: 367–374.

Thomas, D. 1990. Intra-household resource allocation: An inferential approach, *Journal of Human Resources* **25**(4): 635–664.

Thomas, D. 1993. The distribution of income and expenditure within the household, *Annales de Economie et de Statistique* **29**: 109–136.

Thomas, D. 1994. Like father, like son; like mother, like daughter: Parental resources and child height, *Journal of Human Resources* **29**: 950–988.

Thomas, D. and Chen, C.-L. 1993. Income shares and shares of income, *RAND Discussion Paper*, RAND Corporation, Santa Monica, California.

Thomas, D., Lavy, V. and Strauss, J. 1996. Public policy and anthropometric outcomes in the Côte d'Ivoire, *Journal of Public Economics* **61**(2): 155–192.

Thomas, D. and Strauss, J. 1992. Prices, infrastructure, household characteristics and child height, *Journal of Political Economy* **39**(2): 301–331.

Udry, C. 1996. Gender, agricultural production, and the theory of the household, *Journal of Political Economy* **104**(3): 1010–1046.

Ullah, A. 1988. Nonparametric estimation and hypothesis testing in econometric models, *Empirical Economics* **13**: 223–249.

United Nations 2004. World Population Prospects: The 2004 Revisions, Volume III: Analytical Report.

United Republic of Tanzania 2002. Integrated Labour Force Survey 2000/01. Analytical Report.

van Praag, B. and Ferrer-i-Carbonell, A. 2004. *Happiness quantified: A satisfaction calculus approach*, Oxford University Press, Oxford.

Van Praag, B. M. and Warnaar, M. F. 1993. The cost of children and the use of demographic variables in consumer demand, *in* M. R. Rosenzweig and O. Stark (eds), *Handbook of Population and Family Economics*, Vol. 1 of *Handbook of Population and Family Economics*, Elsevier, chapter 6, pp. 241–273.

Varian, H. R. 1992. *Microeconomic analysis*, W.W. Norton & Company, Inc., New York.

Wang, W. and Famoye, F. 1997. Modeling household fertility decisions with generalized Poisson regression, *Journal of Population Economics* **10**: 273–283.

Westoff, C. F. and Bankole, A. 2001. The contraception-fertility link in sub-Saharan Africa and in other developing countries, *DHS Analytical Studies*, ORC Macro, Calverton.

White, H. 1982. Maximum likelihood estimation of misspecified models, *Econometrica* **50**(1): 1–25.

Wilke, R. 2004. Semiparametric estimation of consumption based equivalence scales - The case of Germany, *ZEW Discussion Paper No. 04-53*, ZEW.

Winkelmann, R. and Zimmermann, K. 1995. Recent developments in count data modelling: Theory and application, *Journal of Economic Surveys* **9**: 1–24.

Wooldridge, J. 2002. *Econometric analysis of cross section and panel data*, MIT Press, Cambridge.

Yatchew, A. 1997. An elementary estimator of the partial linear model, *Economics Letters* **57**: 135–143.

Yatchew, A. 1999. An elementary nonparametric differencing test of equality of regression functions, *Economics Letters* **62**: 271–278.

Yatchew, A., Sun, Y. and Deri, C. 2003. Efficient estimation of semiparametric equivalence scales with evidence from South Africa, *Journal of Business & Economic Statistics* **21**(2): 247–57.

Yngstrom, I. 2002. Women, wives and land rights in Africa: Situating gender beyond the household in the debate over land policy and changing tenure systems, *Oxford Development Studies* **30**(1): 21–40.

**Development Economics and Policy**

Series edited by Franz Heidhues, Joachim von Braun and Manfred Zeller

Band 1 Andrea Fadani: Agricultural Price Policy and Export and Food Production in Cameroon. A Farming Systems Analysis of Pricing Policies. The Case of Coffee-Based Farming Systems. 1999.

Band 2 Heike Michelsen: Auswirkungen der Währungsunion auf den Strukturanpassungsprozeß der Länder der afrikanischen Franc-Zone. 1995.

Band 3 Stephan Bea: Direktinvestitionen in Entwicklungsländern. Auswirkungen von Stabilisierungsmaßnahmen und Strukturreformen in Mexiko. 1995.

Band 4 Franz Heidhues / François Kamajou: Agricultural Policy Analysis – Proceedings of an International Seminar, held at the University of Dschang, Cameroon on May 26 and 27 1994, funded by the European Union under the Science and Technology Program (STD). 1996.

Band 5 Elke M. Förster: Protection or Liberalization? A Policy Analysis of the Korean Beef Sector. 1996.

Band 6 Gertrud Schrieder: The Role of Rural Finance for Food Security of the Poor in Cameroon. 1996.

Band 7 Nestor R. Ahoyo Adjovi: Economie des Systèmes de Production intégrant la Culture de Riz au Sud du Bénin: Potentialités, Contraintes et Perspectives. 1996.

Band 8 Jenny Müller: Income Distribution in the Agricultural Sector of Thailand. Empirical Analysis and Policy Options. 1996.

Band 9 Michael Brüntrup: Agricultural Price Policy and its Impact on Production, Income, Employment and the Adoption of Innovations. A Farming Systems Based Analysis of Cotton Policy in Northern Benin. 1997.

Band 10 Justin Bomda: Déterminants de l'Epargne et du Crédit, et leurs Implications pour le Développement du Système Financier Rural au Cameroun. 1998.

Band 11 John M. Msuya: Nutrition Improvement Projects in Tanzania: Implementation, Determinants of Performance, and Policy Implications. 1998.

Band 12 Andreas Neef: Auswirkungen von Bodenrechtswandel auf Ressourcennutzung und wirtschaftliches Verhalten von Kleinbauern in Niger und Benin. 1999.

Band 13 Susanna Wolf (ed.): The Future of EU-ACP Relations. 1999.

Band 14 Franz Heidhues / Gertrud Schrieder (eds.): Romania – Rural Finance in Transition Economies. 2000.

Band 15 Katinka Weinberger: Women's Participation. An Economic Analysis in Rural Chad and Pakistan. 2000.

Band 16 Christof Batzlen: Migration and Economic Development. Remittances and Investments in South Asia: A Case Study of Pakistan. 2000.

Band 17 Matin Qaim: Potential Impacts of Crop Biotechnology in Developing Countries. 2000.

Band 18 Jean Senahoun: Programmes d'ajustement structurel, sécurité alimentaire et durabilité agricole. Une approche d'analyse intégrée, appliquée au Bénin. 2001.

Band 19 Torsten Feldbrügge: Economics of Emergency Relief Management in Developing Countries. With Case Studies on Food Relief in Angola and Mozambique. 2001.

Band 20 Claudia Ringler: Optimal Allocation and Use of Water Resources in the Mekong River Basin: Multi-Country and Intersectoral Analyses. 2001.

Band 21 Arnim Kuhn: Handelskosten und regionale (Des-)Integration. Russlands Agrarmärkte in der Transformation. 2001.

Band 22  Ortrun Anne Gronski: Stock Markets and Economic Growth. Evidence from South Africa. 2001.

Band 23  Patrick Webb / Katinka Weinberger (eds.): Women Farmers. Enhancing Rights, Recognition and Productivity. 2001.

Band 24  Mingzhi Sheng: Lebensmittelkonsum und -konsumtrends in China. Eine empirische Analyse auf der Basis ökonometrischer Nachfragemodelle. 2002.

Band 25  Maria Iskandarani: Economics of Household Water Security in Jordan. 2002.

Band 26  Romeo Bertolini: Telecommunication Services in Sub-Saharan Africa. An Analysis of Access and Use in the Southern Volta Region in Ghana. 2002.

Band 27  Dietrich Müller-Falcke: Use and Impact of Information and Communication Technologies in Developing Countries' Small Businesses. Evidence from Indian Small Scale Industry. 2002.

Band 28  Wolfram Erhardt: Financial Markets for Small Enterprises in Urban and Rural Northern Thailand. Empirical Analysis on the Demand for and Supply of Financial Services, with Particular Emphasis on the Determinants of Credit Access and Borrower Transaction Costs. 2002.

Band 29  Wensheng Wang: The Impact of Information and Communication Technologies on Farm Households in China. 2002.

Band 30  Shyamal K. Chowdhury: Institutional and Welfare Aspects of the Provision and Use of Information and Communication Technologies in the Rural Areas of Bangladesh and Peru. 2002.

Band 31  Annette Luibrand: Transition in Vietnam. Impact of the Rural Reform Process on an Ethnic Minority. 2002.

Band 32  Felix Ankomah Asante: Economic Analysis of Decentralisation in Rural Ghana. 2003.

Band 33  Chodechai Suwanaporn: Determinants of Bank Lending in Thailand: An Empirical Examination for the Years 1992 to 1996. 2003.

Band 34  Abay Asfaw: Costs of Illness, Demand for Medical Care, and the Prospect of Community Health Insurance Schemes in the Rural Areas of Ethiopia. 2003.

Band 35  Gi-Soon Song: The Impact of Information and Communication Technologies (ICTs) on Rural Households. A Holistic Approach Applied to the Case of Lao People's Democratic Republic. 2003.

Band 36  Daniela Lohlein: An Economic Analysis of Public Good Provision in Rural Russia. The Case of Education and Health Care. 2003.

Band 37  Johannes Woelcke. Bio-Economics of Sustainable Land Management in Uganda. 2003.

Band 38  Susanne M. Ziemek: The Economics of Volunteer Labor Supply. An Application to Countries of a Different Development Level. 2003.

Band 39  Doris Wiesmann: An International Nutrition Index. Concept and Analyses of Food Insecurity and Undernutrition at Country Levels. 2004.

Band 40  Isaac Osei-Akoto: The Economics of Rural Health Insurance. The Effects of Formal and Informal Risk-Sharing Schemes in Ghana. 2004.

Band 41  Yuansheng Jiang: Health Insurance Demand and Health Risk Management in Rural China. 2004.

Band 42  Roukayatou Zimmermann: Biotechnology and Value-added Traits in Food Crops: Relevance for Developing Countries and Economic Analyses. 2004.

Band 43  F. Markus Kaiser: Incentives in Community-based Health Insurance Schemes. 2004.

Band 44  Thomas Herzfeld: *Corruption begets Corruption*. Zur Dynamik und Persistenz der Korruption. 2004.

Band 45   Edilegnaw Wale Zegeye: The Economics of On-Farm Conservation of Crop Diversity in Ethiopia: Incentives, Attribute Preferences and Opportunity Costs of Maintaining Local Varieties of Crops. 2004.

Band 46   Adama Konseiga: Regional Integration Beyond the Traditional Trade Benefits: Labor Mobility contribution. The Case of Burkina Faso and Côte d'Ivoire. 2005.

Band 47   Beyene Tadesse Ferenji: The Impact of Policy Reform and Institutional Transformation on Agricultural Performance. An Economic Study of Ethiopian Agriculture. 2005.

Band 48   Sabine Daude: Agricultural Trade Liberalization in the WTO and Its Poverty Implications. A Study of Rural Households in Northern Vietnam. 2005.

Band 49   Kadir Osman Gyasi: Determinants of Success of Collective Action on Local Commons. An Empirical Analysis of Community-Based Irrigation Management in Northern Ghana. 2005.

Band 50   Borbala E. Balint: Determinants of Commercial Orientation and Sustainability of Agricultural Production of the Individual Farms in Romania. 2006.

Band 51   Pamela Marinda: Effects of Gender Inequality in Resource Ownership and Access on Household Welfare and Food Security in Kenya. A Case Study of West Pokot District. 2006.

Band 52   Charles Palmer: The Outcomes and their Determinants from Community-Company Contracting over Forest Use in Post-Decentralization Indonesia. 2006.

Band 53   Hardwick Tchale: Agricultural Policy and Soil Fertility Management in the Maize-based Smallholder Farming System in Malawi. 2006.

Band 54   John Kedi Mduma: Rural Off-Farm Employment and its Effects on Adoption of Labor Intensive Soil Conserving Measures in Tanzania. 2006.

Band 55   Mareike Meyn: The Impact of EU Free Trade Agreements on Economic Development and Regional Integration in Southern Africa. The Example of EU-SACU Trade Relations. 2006.

Band 56   Clemens Breisinger: Modelling Infrastructure Investments, Growth and Poverty Impact. A Two-Region Computable General Equilibrium Perspective on Vietnam. 2006.

Band 57   Meike Wollni: Coping with the Coffee Crisis. An Analysis of the Production and Marketing Performance of Coffee Farmers in Costa Rica. 2007.

Band 58   Franklin Simtowe: Performance and Impact of Microfinance. Evidence from Joint Liability Lending Programs in Malawi. 2008.

Band 59   Xiangping Jia: Credit Rationing and Institutional Constraint. Evidence from Rural China. 2008.

Band 60   Holger Seebens: The Economics of Gender and the Household in Developing Countries. 2009.

www.peterlang.de

Franklin Simtowe

# Performance and Impact of Microfinance

**Evidence from Joint Liability Lending Programs in Malawi**

Frankfurt am Main, Berlin, Bern, Bruxelles, New York, Oxford, Wien, 2008.
XX, 177 pp., num. fig.
Development Economics and Policy.
Series edited by Franz Heidhues and Joachim von Braun. Vol. 58
ISBN 978-3-631-57242-9 · pb. € 39.–*

This study assesses the performance and impact of microfinance from group lending schemes with joint liability in Malawi. The study applies econometric models to technology adoption by farm households and to moral hazard and intra-group risk sharing to address the following objectives: to determine factors influencing the incidence of moral hazard among credit groups, to examine the extent to which intra-group insurance occurs, to investigate its underlying determinants, to assess the impact of households' access to credit on the adoption of hybrid maize among households that vary in their credit constraints, and to assess the effect of credit on risk attitudes. The study recommends a number of microfinance policies as a way of improving performance and impact of microfinance.

*Contents:* Microfinance · Impact Assessment · Food Security · Agricultural Productivity · Solidarity Group Lending

Frankfurt am Main · Berlin · Bern · Bruxelles · New York · Oxford · Wien
Distribution: Verlag Peter Lang AG
Moosstr. 1, CH-2542 Pieterlen
Telefax 00 41 (0) 32 / 376 17 27

*The €-price includes German tax rate
Prices are subject to change without notice
**Homepage http://www.peterlang.de**

www.ingramcontent.com/pod-product-compliance
Ingram Content Group UK Ltd.
Pitfield, Milton Keynes, MK11 3LW, UK
UKHW021836210426
5322IPUK00021B/319